Church-going Insider
or
Gospel-carrying Outsider?

A different view of congregations

Judith McWilliams Dickhart

INSIDER or OUTSIDER? A different view of congregations

Part of the SPLASH! Series of resources,
a program of the ELCA Growth in Excellence in Ministry Project,
funded in part by a grant from Lutheran Brotherhood

Author: Judith McWilliams Dickhart
Editor: Kurt Reichardt
Designer: Gail Gottlund

Consultation Team:

Michael Bennethum
Roy Blumhorst
Sheri Delvin
Judith Dickhart
Patricia Katzenmaier
Sally Simmel
Bob Sitze

The Ripples of the Baptized.

Cover photograph © FPG International by Charly Franklin

ISBN Code No. 0-9636630-2-x

Table of Contents

*When they could not find them [Paul and Silas], they dragged
Jason and some believers before the city authorities, shouting,
"These people who have been turning the world upside down
have come here also. . ."* (Acts 17:6 NRSV)

**To all believers who, in order to turn the world upside down,
are ready to turn the church inside out.**

Foreword

The cover of this book features a depiction of one of non-Euclidean geometry's most fascinating forms, the "Möbius Strip." Named after the 19th century German mathematician, astronomer and topologist August Ferdinand Möbius, this curious surface exploits a remarkable property: one-sidedness. This mathematical curiosity invites exploration because its reality is undeniable while its nature is counter-intuitive. (How can a clearly two-sided object have only one side and one edge?)

The answer, of course, is the half-twist applied to a long strip of paper before its two ends are joined to form a band. This simple adjustment adds a third dimension, — depth, — to a previously two-dimensioned item. This deft turn invites incredulous observers to prove to themselves, in simple logic, that what they had previous thought to be true — "a piece of paper has two sides and several edges" — is no longer true.

In *Inside or Outsider? Church-going Insider or Gospel-carrying Outsider?* Judy Dickhart performs the same kind of simple twist, this time turning our notions about "church" and "pastor" and "members" so that the resultant picture is completely different. Counter to our previous intuitions, Judy demonstrates a new single-sidedness — a new kind of unifying look — about Christian congregations. "What would happen," she seems to ask, "if we played with descriptions of inside/outside and were willing to find deeper answers that could make congregations stronger?"

She sets up and then knocks off its perch the kind of dualism that has separated members from clergy, "inside leaders" from "inactive outsiders". She provides a new logic of proving that the "inside church" is best served by tracing our mind's eye along its "outside edge." She helps us examine more logically our small-minded notions that "what's out there" isn't worth examining "in here." And she holds up for our examination the paradox that a congregation focused on its "outsidedness" will grow stronger inside.

Judy isn't a scientist by training, but her trained eye has made her a "topographer" and "astronomer" of the church for over thirty years. A denominational staff member of the former Lutheran Church in America and later, the Evangelical Lutheran Church in America, Judy has worked effectively at the causes of parish renewal and congregational planning and visioning. She has examined the church from close up, seeing the lay of the land and offering specific suggestions for congregations to come alive. She has also gazed into the distant reaches of ecclesiology and described a hopeful, bright future for congregations.

Insider or Outsider? intrigues me, and give me courage in my work as a congregation-renewer. Judy Dickhart's wisdom compels me to seek God's own twists of logic and ends-joining. Her writing in this book delights my soul and gives me hope that Christian congregations will find new life and energy for God's mission.

–Bob Sitze, author
(Not) Trying Too Hard: New Basics for Sustainable Congregations

Introduction

About this book ...

This book's title is not a trick question. It suggests two different mission directions congregations may take. The choice between the two makes a world of difference.

If I were to turn the title into a forced-choice question on a survey entitled *"Advancing The Mission of the Church"*, people who fill out the form would throw their hands up in frustration.

What kind of members should congregations be developing?
(A) Church-going insiders; or
(B) Gospel-carrying outsiders.

"Impossible," those surveyed leaders would say. "You did not construct the question properly. There should be a third choice. The right answer is: (C) Both of the above."

In truth, they would be correct. Nurturing God's people — both gathered and scattered — is important. In practice, however, I believe congregations do not choose both (a) and (b). Rather, almost all their attention is put on (a): developing active, involved church-goers. Leaders may hope that what happens inside a church will rub off on members, but they do not use the time inside to prepare members to carry the Gospel into the world.

In fact, members have come to expect *the church* to be the locus for mission, not *the world*. Many leave worship believing they have fulfilled the church's expectations of them. They are pretty much on their own to figure out how to lead a Christian life the rest of the week. Some would be surprised to hear me describe them as Gospel-carrying outsiders, but they are. And they could be even better at Gospel-carrying with a little inside support. That they don't receive it is the problem.

1

The church has been a comfortable, well-loved home place for me as long as I can remember. Most of my professional life has been spent working for congregations or in denominational offices. I've helped design programs, train consultants and publish studies — all in the hope of advancing God's mission for the church.

But today I see congregations stuck in place. Most are operating in ways that differ little from those used 40 years ago. Congregations may not have changed much, but their place in North American culture has. Today, they operate from the edges, not from the center of society as churches did four decades ago. While there is some merit in being familiar and steadfast, that stability does not make congregations more effective mission centers in the thoroughly secular world of the 21st century. Some congregations have made changes and offer more choices in worship, programs and services. But these new options are often based on time-honored models of organizing, scheduling and setting leadership roles. As with the programs I designed years ago, the new models work on the inside and seek to attract more insiders. Yet church-going insiders continue to be a shrinking segment of North American society. The church seems to be making little difference in the world.

I believe that we church-goers are one of the reasons the church is stuck in place. We imagine our congregations only from the inside. Think about it. When we consider the utility or beauty of our church buildings, we're thinking *inside* the boundaries set by property lines. When we plan worship schedules or changes in worship patterns, chances are we're thinking of how these will work *inside* the sanctuary or fellowship hall, or on the church lawn. When we discuss education programs, we're imagining when and where these can be conducted *inside* the church building. Even when we develop evangelism strategies, we are talking about ways to draw new people *inside* our familiar space and practices.

...we church-goers are one of the reasons the church is stuck in place.

We concentrate on developing church-going insiders: Christians who come into our church buildings often, learn our church language and rituals, and conform to the ways we do things in our congregation. The more insiders our congregations have, the more successful we are. Isn't that how the reasoning goes? But does that fulfill God's mission for the church, or does it simply follow good practices to preserve the institution? Is the church an instrument of God's mission, or the object of that mission?

The church's traditional mission strategy has been a one location, one-day-a-week, Christian-to-Christian approach, in spite of all the week night activities and other exceptions you might list. If we want congregations to have more influence in the world 20 years from now, we need to reconsider that strategy. I believe that a better approach would take into account other locations, the remaining six weekdays, and all the outsiders with whom church-goers have daily contact. When will it finally dawn on us that we have many more opportunities to deliver the Good News to those without faith if we send it outside the church with Gospel-carrying Christians?

We keep trying to do mission from inside church buildings. That's not where most of the action is. If we really want to reach more people in God's beloved world, we should put as much energy into recognizing Christians as Gospel-carrying outsiders as we do in cultivating them as church-going insiders. In other words:

- Our focus needs to expand from what happens *in* church to include what happens *after* church.

- Our understanding of mission needs to grow beyond what we do *inside* church until it embrace things we do *outside* — sometimes with others and sometimes alone.

- We need to recognize that congregational ministries are carried out not only *inside* by our corporate actions, but also are richly extended by our member's individual actions in *outside* places.

- We need to re-draw congregational boundary lines — from *inside* the church property and its nearby environs — to include all the *outside* places that members inhabit throughout the week. That is where God's mission sends us.

■ Our time together *inside* needs to equip, encourage and sustain us for mission in the world *outside*.

This does not mean making insistent demands that members invite neighbors to church or overtly testify in their workplaces. That usually produces feelings of guilt or incompetence. Rather, I am proposing that congregational leaders pay attention to the worldly places members occupy, help church-goers connect Sunday faith to everyday experience, and celebrate all the ways they serve God in their daily places. In the course of serving God daily, members may invite others to church. Wonderful! Even then the focus needs to remain on carrying the Gospel outside, in order to make a difference in the world.

The question I keep asking is "How could we do things differently *inside* to better carry God's love outside?" Our life together in congregations is the one world over which we Christians have some control. How can we shape our time together to give members more confidence and courage to be Gospel-carriers into weekday places over which they have very little control?

The answers I've found to date are described in this book's seven chapters. They are grouped in three sections or "ideas" that could provide the basis for new congregational mission strategies. Any congregation — no matter its size, circumstances or resources — can adapt these. We insiders are accustomed to thinking about our congregations in terms of numbers and building spaces, financial assets and trained leaders. Granted those resources are important, but they have become limitations, also. If we could see the church differently, we might find untapped resources and alternate ways to advance God's mission. That could make all the difference in the world.

1st Idea: Make the most of different perspectives.

2nd Idea: Re-think ideas taken-for-granted.

3rd Idea: Start with simple changes.

Prelude:

Two views of the river

We chose our retirement home because of the view. From its screened porch, we could see the waters of a small, tidal river. What a great, serene place to sit and read! The porch had room for our favorite rocking chairs, a corner for the round supper table, sky lights and ceiling hooks for summering house plants — even space for a day bed piled with pillows. I could imagine how it would look from the first moment I saw it.

Then our grandchildren arrived. What they saw was the narrow beach revealed when the tide was out. What a grand, ever-changing place to play! They have been teaching me to see our home from their perspective. It has become a place with bamboo fishing poles in the garage and night crawlers in the refrigerator. There are lanterns for moonlight picnics at the river's edge, piles of old towels for wiping off river "muck", and a borrowed canoe for exploring the marshes. Occasionally, sandcastles dominate the little beach and collections of shells decorate benches. I never would have imagined!

Not that we hadn't given thought to our children and grandchildren when we decided to move. We calculated routes and mileage. We made sure there were plenty of sleeping spaces for family and friends. But I did not visualize our home as might a child of six or nine. I had not considered what would be appealing or attractive to them; I did not see with their eyes.

Neither had I considered that our place might be a learning lab for children who think snakes are "cool" on Animal Planet but have never met one in the back yard, or who are familiar with swimming pools but unaccustomed to tidal currents. Nor had I expected it to be a quiet retreat away from urban noise and unrelenting schedules for their parents, a place where they would invite neighbors to join them for weekends. I just thought they would come to celebrate special occasions, and enjoy the love and support of family. While they do, there is more. They come to get away from daily routine, and to do things they don't do at home. Usually they return refreshed, and occasionally they return with some new knowledge tucked away. I never would have imagined.

I'm learning to see our retirement place differently. What would happen if we church-goers could see our congregations with other sets of eyes? We householders furnish our churches with our valued activities, in settings we make comfortable. What might change if we re-examined ideas and habits we take for granted? What if the church became a lab to nourish and equip Gospel-carriers, as well as a retreat place for nurturing church-goers? Imagine it!

1st idea:
Make the most of different perspectives

Chapter 1

Recognize other perspectives

This book revolves around one simple, un-easy question. "How could we do things differently inside to better carry God's love outside?"

My first answer is the one I learned from my grandchildren: *recognize and respect the fact that pastors and lay members see their congregations from different perspectives.* People see the church differently because they have unique histories with, and connections to, it. If we pay attention to differences in perspective we give credibility to both lay and clergy viewpoints. We also open the door to new insights that could turn into better ways to do things inside our congregations.

Consider the notion of perspective itself by observing two artists at work.

Painters across Museum Square

Imagine an artist standing at an easel in the center of a public square, drawing a picture of a famous museum. The artist is transferring a certain perspective of that museum onto canvas. One of the marks of a good painter is the ability to show depth on the canvas's flat surface. To do that, the artist looks at the subject from different angles, perhaps making sketches to get a better feel for the whole subject. Finally, the artist chooses a particular view of the museum and commits that sight to canvas.

Imagine a second artist drawing the same museum, but working at an easel farther down — near a corner of the square. Soon there will be two pictures that show the same building, but with noticeable differences. If they are good artists with similar styles, observers should be able to recognize the sameness even as they point out the differences. The second painting makes both drawings more interesting.

Seeing things from different perspectives is fairly easy when it involves tangible objects or experiences. Standing at the podium provides a different view of the audience than sitting in the back row. It also prompts different emotions, even as does viewing familiar roads when one is flying in a small prop plane. Think about lab experiments in a chemistry class, or walking over a Civil War battlefield. When people actually see familiar things from different vantage points – with eyes and hearts wide open – it deepens their understanding of other people, places and experiences.

Intangible objects are not as easy to see from differing angles. I imagine them with my "mind's eye", try to sketch them, and convey them to you through word pictures. But I cannot be certain that my words capture the depth of the object or show it in its wholeness.

Views of the church ...

When I use the term "church" in this book, I am thinking of congregations — local communities of believers. Certainly, the church is manifested also through denominations and global organizations. It is an institution with a long history, and the gathering of saints in the church triumphant. There are many ways to imagine the church. But in these pages, I am concentrating on "church" as most readers know it best – the congregations to which you and I belong.

"Come," a friend says, "let me show you my church." It is one thing to walk through a building as my friend points out offices and classrooms or we stand quietly in the sanctuary. These are real, tangible places. It is quite another matter for that friend to describe the community of Christians who congregate there. So many things about congregations are intangible: beliefs, history, traditions and norms, patterns of relationships. How does our friend put those into words? Congregations are much more than buildings, but their invisible qualities are not so easy to describe.

Before looking at the church from *other* perspectives, please recognize that congregations are not easily defined from *any* perspective. Beyond blueprints and property lines, all descriptions rely upon intangibles. Some people try to describe churches by referring to constitutions, pastorates, affiliations and 75th anniversary booklets. Others measure them with statistics and program profiles. Scholars try to explain the church theologically or sociologically. All of these factors contribute to our understanding, but congregations are more than the sum of their parts.

Because congregations are communities of believers in specific places and times, all definitions are conditional. Because they are gatherings of unique people with their own faith journeys, each congregation looks a bit different from any other. Individual congregations look different from the inside, too. The word pictures I might use to describe my congregation will not match exactly the pictures other members might sketch. Even though we belong to the same church and may have a lot of other things in common, we see our congregations through our own experiences and histories.

Church insiders will be freer to look at congregations from other perspectives, if they recognize that:

- Everyone sees the church through the lenses of their own experiences and circumstances.
- Personal perspectives give flat views because they show the church from only one angle – that of those who share the same vantage point.
- Personal perspectives gain depth when they see the viewpoints of others who look at the church from different angles.
- Conversations about the church become more intelligible when words carry clear, common understanding.
- The more that is shared from different perspectives, the deeper and truer the picture of "church" becomes.

Exploring from differing perspectives promises widened horizons which show things in ways never before imagined.

Two simple perspectives ...

While I won't be able to explore many perspectives in this small book, I can outline two examples of basic angles from which Christians look at the church. They can provide a framework to use in the future. The first is from the pastor's place; the second is from the place of lay members. Of course, each provides a broad generalization. The first one doesn't take into account associate pastors and other professional staff whose views differ from senior pastors. It doesn't differentiate between pastors of small congregations, city congregations, old or new congregations. The list of variations in laity perspectives is even longer than that for clergy.

While both over-simplify, limiting the number of perspectives at this point makes it easier to demonstrate the basic idea that pastors and laity see the church from different places. Once that is clear, you can explore the differences between the perceptions of senior pastors of large suburban congregations and part-time pastors of small country congregations. Or the differences between lay members who serve on committees, and those who only come to worship once or twice a month.

Remember, these two perspectives are *brief descriptions* which do not consider the uniqueness of individual pastors, laity or congregations. Also, *they are not judgments.* One perspective is not right and the other wrong. My goal in identifying them is to recognize that different perspectives exist, and that those differences may tell you why some things are working well in your congregations while others are not. They may hold clues to exciting possibilities or unmet needs, unreal expectations or emerging conflicts.

There are two questions you might ask yourself as you read through the descriptions.

- Does this ring true to my experience?
- What is significant about these differences?

I am working from the premise that perspective is shaped by the *activities* that dominate a person's time in the *places* he or she frequents. Daily occupations and their locations do not fully explain why people see things as they do. Family heritage, past experience and other factors contribute as well, but to keep this simple, I want to concentrate on the influence of *activity* and *place* in defining perspective. Using those two factors, I can describe the vantage point from which pastors see their congregations, and you can compare that view with the perspective of lay members.

Insiders with two different viewpoints

Pastors look from the inside-center ...

Many of the *activities* that occupy the pastors' time are congregational: leading worship, teaching new member classes, attending church council and committee meetings, preparing newsletter and bulletin copy, supporting youth ministry, providing pre-marital counseling, supervising room set-ups for various activities. And that's just the beginning of the list. Add to it the preparation time that backs up the pastor's activities.

By design, pastors are their congregation's most active members. That's what their congregations expect of them. They may not be directly involved with everything that goes on, but they have the broadest knowledge of congregational activities. The congregation is on their minds seven days a week. Many are engaged in congregational activities six, and sometimes seven, days each week. It is their call, their living.

In addition, most congregational activities take *place* in church buildings. Some pastors may have offices at home, but when the action begins, their place is at the church. If the church building contains an office, members expect to find their pastor there during certain weekday hours.

The place where pastors interact with members is usually the church building. While pastors visit members and prospective members at home, see them in the hospital, accompany groups on service projects or to community meetings and sports outings, most pastors see most members most often at church. Again, that's by design and expectation. It's the way congregations operate.

Pastors have personal interests that take them to other places. They are spouses, parents, neighbors and citizens, and have hobbies and recreational activities. Nevertheless, the perspective of pastors is strongly influenced by being literally and figuratively inside the church most of their working hours. (Note: In Chapter 5 we'll consider further the importance of the pastor's whole life.)

Finally, pastors are more likely than most members to have dreams about what their congregations might accomplish if stretched to their full potential. They are rarely satisfied with the status quo. Some may feel challenged by leaders to make their congregations successful, but much of the challenge comes from within each pastor. Again, this is their call, their living.

With most of their activities placed in the church building, pastors see the congregation as a community gathered together. Within this gathered community members worship faithfully, and give of their time, money and talents both to nurture growth inside and to serve the needy outside. Pastors want their congregations to be dynamic, challenging communities. They encourage members to lead Christian lives when they scatter back to their homes, schools, places of work and recreation.

Lay members look from the outside-in ...

Most *activities* that occupy the time of the church's remaining members have little to do with the congregation's weekly schedule. Lay members are busy going to school, seeking employment, pursuing careers or redefining themselves in retirement. Managing these activities is on their minds seven days a week. Many spend six days each week in their work places, and for some Sunday is a workday, too. They may not see their work as a call; they do see it as earning a living.

For most members, time spent in congregational activities is limited. Weekly worship, a monthly committee meeting and choir practice probably qualifies one as an "active" member. That amounts to roughly five or six hours weekly. While some spend twice that amount of time fitting church activities into busy schedules, it is still far less time than the attention most active members devote each week to earning their living or on daily household activities.

Day-to-day contact with fellow members is limited, too. Though others in their family, neighborhood or at work may also be members, the weekday time they share usually is not related to congregational activity. For many lay members, most people with whom they spend most of their time have no connection to their congregations.

If much of their daily activity is not church-related, it follows that the *places* lay people frequent are outside the church building: school and work places, homes, neighborhoods and volunteer places. Even the most active members do not come to church as often as the pastor does. Going to the church is not a daily activity unless members are church secretaries, work in the nursery school or have other occupations they pursue in the building.

The daily places of lay members may be supportive, indifferent or hostile to the Christian faith. Members look for ways to do their work in environments that are comfortable and in keeping with their faith. Some may see their work as an extension of their church activity; many see it as separate. Their daily lives are spent outside the church. Church is a place they go on certain occasions. The perspective of lay people is strongly influenced by being literally — if not figuratively — outside the church.

Finally, lay members are more likely than their pastors to want to retain the congregation's status quo. Church is one place in their stressed, changing lives that offers steadiness and reliability. This does not mean that they will not support some innovation. They want their congregations to be better and stronger. But radical change or controversy is not appealing. That disrupts relationships, takes energy, and threatens the continuity they seek in their gathered community of believers. They want the church to offer comfort to help them through the week as they try to make a living.

With most of their activities away from the church building, lay members see the congregation as a belonging group with whom they gather occasionally for support, spiritual nourishment and doing good works. They want their congregations to continue to be stable, comfortable places. They have some sense of responsibility for their church, but recognize it as one of many demands on their time, money and talents. Their lives are focused on doing their daily work well. Scattered in the world, members try to carry out Christian ideals in their personal lives, but see little connection between their church membership and their daily tasks.

Two insider perspectives

Clergy	Lay members
Their daily living is occupied with congregational activities.	Their daily living is occupied with schoolwork, working for employers or themselves, or with retirement activities.
They are in the church building almost every day, with some time spent in the surrounding communities.	They are at work places in their communities daily, with some occasional time spent in the church building.
Most of the people with whom they have daily contact are church members, church officials or are interested in joining a church.	Few of the people with whom they have daily contact are members of their congregation, and they may or may not be Christians.
They conduct their daily work in an environment supportive of the congregation's life and mission.	They conduct their daily work in environments that are neutral or even hostile to Christianity and the mission of the church.
They sense that God calls them to their daily work.	Many see little connection between daily work and being a church member.
They imagine some changes in the congregation as a result of doing their daily work.	They look for stability in their congregations to support them in their daily work.
They see the congregation primarily as a community gathered in worship, giving, nurturing and serving.	They see the congregation as an occasional gathering place in the midst of their busy, scattered daily lives.

Comparing the two perspectives …

These two perspectives illustrate that clergy and laity see congregations from different vantage points. Since the particulars of each perspective are open to challenge and change, I invite your modifications.

The first point of comparison is *activities*. What things do clergy and laity do inside the church? The pastor serves members at life's significant moments — such as birth, marriage, illness and death. Pastors are more likely to initiate actions aimed at fulfilling the congregation's purpose, be held accountable for growth or decline in membership and financial resources, and are usually the ones who soothe members upset by changes in the church.

Laity inside the church could be described as the "supporting cast" arrayed around the pastor's central role. Lay members take responsibilities as planners and decision-makers, teaching staff, altar guild members, or committee and small group leaders. They look after the property, take flowers to shut-ins and prepare fellowship meals. They assist pastors in worship by reading lessons, ushering and singing in the choir. They work together in ways that build upon and extend the pastor's efforts.

What kinds of things do clergy and laity do outside the church? They engage in similar activities in the course of their personal lives: caring for families, maintaining households, saying "hello" to neighbors. But when it comes to their work lives, there is a big difference. Clergy go *inside* to engage in activities familiar to all pastors and moderately familiar to most lay people. Laity, on the other hand, stay *outside* to engage in activities that are often unfamiliar to clergy and to other lay people. They carry on a wide variety of activities using an impressive diversity of skills, with little attention from their congregations.

The second point of comparison is *place* — how laity and clergy connect to the church building. Lay people come and go, but the pastor comes and stays. The pastor has the keys to all the locked places in the building, and knows where things are kept and all the light switch locations. Some lay people do, too. Some are at home in the church, and are part of that wonderful supporting cast that willingly gives its full attention to the church's programs and property as soon as they cross the boundary between their daily lives and their common church life.

Clergy are called to lead and serve inside the church. Meanwhile, lay people are *occupied* in the outside world, not in the church. Outside is where they earn their living, exercise their gifts and live out their baptisms. What they do outside is valuable both to society and God's mission.

Lay people *should* spend most of their time away from church buildings. They have unique opportunities that clergy will never have to serve God outside. Their place outside the church is a good thing, to be respected and valued.

Despite all the differences in clergy and laity perspectives, both groups care deeply about their congregation's welfare. When lay people come to church, they expect to concentrate on church matters. They come from different places but they are united as church-going insiders. They focus on the pastor's workplace. Their own workplaces receive little notice in church meetings. Much of their outside knowledge and contacts with outsiders go unrecognized. Think about that.

Those perspectives meet on Tuesday and Sunday

Pastors spend many work hours in the church place. During some of those, lay people come inside to plan for or participate in various activities. At such times, clergy and laity apply their different views to common interests. Consider how these two perspectives link up inside.

On Tuesday nights ...

Think about that monthly committee meeting scheduled for Tuesday at 7:30 P.M. Assume the pastor and committee chair have consulted about the agenda, that a reminder mailing with the agenda enclosed was distributed at least a week before, and that all committee members are expected to be present.

- ■ Who will have taken the most time to prepare for the meeting?
- ■ Whose daily life is more likely to be affected by decisions made during the meeting?
- ■ Where will actions be implemented – inside or outside the church building?

The questions show the impact of Tuesday's meeting on its partici-pants. They also illustrate why the clergy's insider perspective may receive more attention during the meeting. The pastor's work time is like-ly to be more affected than the time of other meeting participants. Pas-tors see Tuesday evening meetings as an extension of their daily occupa-tion. Lay members do not; church is not their work place.

Committees and work groups composed of laity constitute one way churches have planned program activities for generations. Pastors often come to meetings better prepared than many committee members because the committee activity is related to the pastor's work goals. Mem-bers expect pastors to have suggestions about forthcoming activities. They may defer to those ideas rather than try to articulate their own. Not surprisingly, the Tuesday meeting accomplishments usually have more impact on the pastor's daily life. That's because — in the operating model that congregations follow — church activities are part of the pastor's daily work.

This doesn't mean that lay people come to meetings unprepared. Many devote an amazing amount of effort carrying out their committee responsibilities. They come to the meetings, however, from a different place. The meeting agenda is not likely to be related to the work they have done during the day, nor will the actions that result. Lay members have to make a mental and emotional shift from the goals, tasks, concerns and relationships that have occupied them all day. They are entering a new environment. The pastor is not.

Lay members fit congregational activity around their dominant daily activities. Sometimes this means skipping dinner. I've been in more than one meeting where Charlie stopped at home after work just long enough to pick up papers before coming to the church. Or Lilian came directly after seeing her last patient. Faithful lay leaders like Charlie and Lilian do this willingly because the congregation is important to them. They give time and attention to what this committee is trying to accomplish, but the next day they will be back in other environments that will absorb their attention and energy. Lay members take on some limited assign-ments between meetings but do not devote as much time to church pro-grams as do their pastors.

Again on Sundays …

In some ways, going to church on Sunday is the same. Pastors in their work places, and lay members who are not, both bring their views of church with them. Both have opinions about how worship should be conducted, and what kind of education and fellowship should take place.

While pastors are concentrating on worship, education and fellowship, lay people are looking forward to being refreshed by all three. Unlike clergy, coming to church allows them to leave their daily occupations behind. It takes them into an environment full of people of faith. Since everyone there believes in Christ, it is a safe place in which to express faith and be open in worshiping God. That's different from many lay people's daily environment.

Sunday is the most crucial workday for pastors. They know that is the time they'll have contact with more members and prospective members than any other day of the week. Some lay members would be surprised to know how much stress this produces! Few of them have preached a sermon once, let alone week after week. Few will hear comments about un-singable hymns, or the squirming four-year-old in the last pew. Most will not have to find the key to the Sunday school closet, worry about snow on the sidewalks, or explain that the guest speaker for the adult forum is ill.

Lay people do not understand all the Sunday pressures pastors experience. They do know that this is their easiest chance to communicate face-to-face with their pastors without making time for an appointment during the week. Sunday is their best time to exchange information and deal with details related to their church responsibilities. Because pastors have so many things to do on Sundays, however, they can't always give the individual attention members might expect. While greeting people after worship, pastors may not remember that someone mentioned changing a meeting time They may not grasp the significance of brief comments about relatives who are ill or layoffs at work.

Sunday becomes a time to critique how things are going at church, to do planning and to recruit people for church responsibilities. While it really may not be a good time for those activities – because both clergy and laity have other things on their minds – it is the one time of the week most members will see each other. Matters not attended to on one Sunday often are put off to the next Sunday.

In short, clergy and laity have learned to focus on the church despite the different places it claims in their daily lives. Pastors expect to take a leadership role, and are expected to oversee the execution of decisions, plans and programs. Their place is at church. Laity expects to take limited leadership roles, and are expected to handle specific, volunteer tasks. They make space in their weekday places to prepare for or participate in church activities. Sunday is the church day of the week. More is expected of the pastor on that day than any other. Members have the most contact and interaction with the pastor and with fellow members on that day. This is the way Christians who come from different viewpoints have learned to work together to build up the church.

That is the problem

So, what is wrong with this picture? Three things.

First, focusing solely on the church diminishes the importance of all that goes on outside the church. When I described the Tuesday evening meeting, I emphasized the adjustment that lay people make — setting aside significant parts of their lives — when they come inside. Most congregations that I have known do little to encourage members to share their daily concerns or accomplishments in any significant way.

Therefore when people come inside, they don't always feel free to talk about outside issues. When and how does the church address real issues besides illness and death? I remember interviewing a group of divorced mothers. The church was the *last* place they felt they could turn to in their despair and humiliation. They did not see their congregations as places of support. What happens when members are struggling with divorce, unemployment, substance abuse, financial reversals, problem neighbors or children, job pressures or ethical issues in the workplace? Is it enough that the pastor is available for counseling? Could there be other ways to demonstrate compassion for worldly matters inside the church? Congregations who pay attention to both church and world concerns make their churches safer places for members. Imagine that!

Secondly, keeping the focus inside drastically limits the church's ability to minister. Pastors cannot be sympathetic toward, or offer guidance for, couples who are splitting up if they don't know this is happening to member families. If they are not aware of these worldly needs, program planners cannot provide training for people who need parenting skills, or social services for members suddenly laid off from work. The church's agenda will be an inside agenda unless some attention is consciously diverted to the daily places of members; that means cultivating the habit of thinking both inside and outside when members gather. Congregations that are near-sighted need to become bi-focal.

The church is the pastor's work place. As in other work places, it can consume the worker's attention and block out surrounding places. A few years ago, I worked in a second floor office whose window looked out onto a strand of maple trees. It was a beautiful sight and I found it very easy to concentrate there. It was almost like having a tree-house office retreat. In the fall when the trees lost their leaves, my view changed. I could see the street with vehicles rushing uphill and down. The busy, noisy road had been there all along, but I had been able to ignore it — even block the sounds from my mind.

All of us who work inside the church risk focusing so much on our immediate surroundings that we cease hearing the traffic outside. The great gift that lay members can offer their pastors is their view from the edge. They look in at the church from the roadway. They also look out to the road's intersections and forks. Pastors need to ask members to describe the view from the edge. Lay members need to tell  pastors stories from beyond the property lines, without waiting to be asked.

Finally, having a designated church day isolates Sunday from the other days God created. It may give lay people the illusion that they have fulfilled their Christian obligations by going to church on Sunday. Unless church language and actions on Sundays shine light on what God is doing the other six days of the week in other places, the connection between church life inside and daily life outside will be dim. It does not need to be that way.

While lay people literally leave their daily environments behind when they come to church, they bring the issues and pressures of those environments with them. They rejoice that their children are OK as they sing the first hymn, think about problems at work during the sermon, worry about Aunt Anne during The Prayers. Daily life seeps into Sunday life. Lay members are looking for ways to express thanks that God sustained them last week. They're listening for words of wisdom and encouragement to get them through next week. Clergy who are in touch with their outside lives can provide those words.

For many lay members, the church is the place where they can be comfortable worshiping God and sharing their faith. It is a place to forge friendships with like-minded people, and a community in which to teach children Christian values. It might be a place where they could share everyday concerns, and figure out how to share their faith with people in their daily places. When congregations begin to think of members as Gospel-carrying outsiders, the role of the church changes. It becomes the support system that helps people through the ups and downs of life, and the training center that equips them to be God's representatives every day of the week.

Insider-Thinking:
Diminishes the importance of all that goes on outside the church.
Limits the church's ability to minister.
Isolates Sunday from the other days God created.

Chapter 2

Value different views

"How could we do things differently inside to better carry God's love outside?" My second answer to the question may seem risky: *by welcoming differences and harnessing the energy tension produces.*

Pastors and laity gain an understanding of their differences when they compare their perspectives. I believe that it is understanding those perspectives — and the tensions implied — that may prove to be most beneficial within congregations. I wish we would explore differences in perspective until we hear more and more members saying "I never thought about it that way." That could make all the difference in the world for carrying out the church's mission!

One of my favorite examples of making the most of tension comes from the story of Helen Keller, who was left deaf and blind by a childhood illness.

Seeing W-A-T-E-R

William Gibson's The Miracle Worker[1] *dramatizes the tug-of-war between young Helen and her teacher, Annie Sullivan. It's a powerful story of using tension imaginatively. In the play, Annie struggles to teach the belligerent child to communicate despite Helen's being deaf and blind. In the last scene, the two of them are re-filling the water pitcher Helen had thrown at Annie across the dinner table moments before. Annie spells w-a-t-e-r into Helen's hand as they pump the water from the well. She has done this many times before. But this time is different. The miracle happens. Helen suddenly understands that the finger-tracings in her hand name the water she is feeling. The moment Helen Keller connected the abstract word "water" with the real, wet stuff pouring from the pump, her world changed.*

Instantly, she understood the connection between two sets of familiar things. One set was the alphabet that Annie Sullivan had been teaching her. The second was a collage of tangible everyday things she touched, smelled and tasted. The notion that these two sets of things were related to each other was astounding to Helen. It gave her a way to perceive her silent, sightless world.

Think of the energy that released. Instead of being consumed by fighting each other, teacher and student could devote themselves to learning. They thrived on it. They found joy in themselves and the roles they played. Helen and Annie finally used the tension between them to their benefit.

Couldn't the same benefits accrue as lay people and pastors use the tension created by their different perspectives as a force for renewal? The pastor's viewpoint meets the lay member's perspective on Tuesday evening, Sunday morning and other occasions. Those "meetings" sometimes produce burdensome tensions for congregations — destructive when individuals are demeaned or groups become divided, but potentially a tool for positive change, also. Tension can be used constructively to build respect for individuals, as well as stronger relationships within communities. Congregations in which many views are expressed are stronger than ones dominated by one-dimensional views.

Room for Tension

Physical fitness experts remind us that we should welcome tension in exercise. Weight-resistance, elevated heartbeats, and certain kinds of muscle soreness are signs of a good workout. Therapists and psychologists explain the positive value of facing problems and confronting stressful situations. Some businesses report that workers created better products because their design teams thrashed out differences. The notion that tension can be positive sounds fine. But most congregations I know do not welcome differences among members, and they work hard to smooth over tensions.

Differences invite tension ...

If differing views did not get in their way, people might never explore the perspectives of others. I could list all the benefits of doing that, and still not be able to motivate congregational leaders to take time to share their perspectives. Yet, something what irritates them will start an often heated and judgmental exchange of views. In church communities, members will behave at times in a manner that challenges or upsets another's image of their common life. During a congregational meeting, for example, someone may propose a change in the Sunday worship schedule to accommodate parents of young children. That raises uncomfortable questions about the participation of children with adults in worship. Or someone criticizes the pastor for spending more time visiting members than prospective members, opening a discussion about expectations of the pastoral role.

Tensions often build over different perspectives. Adrenaline stokes some people's desire to impose their views on others, to convince or insist on having their way. Differences of opinion become a competition between who will be winners or losers. Consider situations in four kinds of communities:

- Two neighbors have different rules about their children playing in the street.

- The older sister believes it best to maintain her aging father in his own home; her younger sister wants to place him in an assisted care facility.

- One community group sees shopping malls as a threat to Main Street merchants and a source of increasing traffic congestion. A second group is looking for more choices in accessible shopping. A third views new retail chains as a source of economic and employment opportunity.

- The property committee believes it is important to keep attractive grounds with the church's lawn cut, shrubs trimmed and flowers blooming. The kitchen committee views the remodeled kitchen as a place to be used for traditional congregational events, with everything polished and in place between times. The social ministry committee wants to provide a neighborhood latchkey program for 6- to 12-year-olds that includes time for study, play (indoors and out) and supper.

Imagine how each of these situations plays out. Children coaxed into playing ball in the street, then punished by parents. One daughter feeling burdened because her sister won't see what's best for dad. Angry letters to the editor. A divided vote in the congregation council's meeting.

One consequence of having different perspectives can be conflict. I was raised to believe conflict is bad. So were a lot of other people. They learned to appear agreeable, and to smooth things over rather than voice contrary opinions — for arguments might heat up and people would be hurt.

There's truth to that, but not the whole truth. Each of the situations above could have different endings.

- Parents could work out common rules for playing in the street.
- Daughters might find a home care nursing service.
- The town could develop a plan that addresses concerns of the various groups.
- The congregation council could find ways to be good stewards of their inside resources while meeting outside needs.

The whole truth is that different perspectives generate tension, and tension can be draining or invigorating. It can diminish or bring new life. If congregations are to use differences constructively, however, they probably need better ways to voice opinions and influence decision-making. Taking votes or deferring to the opinions of recognized leaders suppresses other "minority" viewpoints, other perspectives. Churches need to be safe places for expressing ideas, even ill-formed ones. Members need practice in thinking "out loud", and in listening patiently.

Pressure of prevailing views from traditional roles

The notion that sharing perspectives could benefit congregations is not a radical idea, but it is not one widely practiced. Whose opinions hold sway in the congregations you know? If your experience is similar 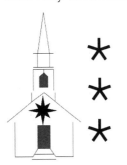 to mine, the people we're both thinking of now are pastors and certain lay leaders. Their views have become more influential because they have more opportunities to voice them, and more power to turn them into actions. As long as they share the same general ideas about what their congregations should be doing, their views about the church are likely to dominate.

Prevailing views have a way of shutting down dialogue and inhibiting people who do not share the same opinions. This isn't a criticism of congregational leaders. It's an observation about one of the habits of church life that keeps congregations stuck in place. Pew sitters have been content to let the preachers do the talking. Pastors have accepted that role. Lay leaders have found ways to exert their influence behind the scenes. The whole congregation is party to keeping the church on the same steady course it's been traveling for years.

Not surprisingly, new members join congregations whose interests and values are similar to their own, thus reinforcing the status quo. People expect groups to which they belong to continue the activities that drew them into membership. A person who joins the local Audubon Society expects to go bird-watching, not to sit through a series of lectures on indigenous wildflowers. If a landscape architect accepts a job offer because the firm says it shares his concerns for the environment, he expects their work policies to reflect that concern.

Members expect others in their belonging groups to behave predictably, to act next week just as they did last year. The coach will be consistent during practice and in enforcing team rules. If Aunt Sue has brought potato salad to the family re-union for the last five years, her sisters expect her to bring it this summer, too. It would upset the menu balance if she showed up with baked beans this time. Very early in their life, groups establish behavior norms that they are slow to change later.

Therefore, even though clergy and laity look at congregations from different perspectives, they both see those things their congregations have been doing for a long time, and roles that have been shaped over generations. Their expectations about church activities and member behavior are based on past experiences. They make plans for future activities that carry on current activities. They assign or accept responsibility for those activities with images in mind of those who have filled such roles before. Congregations are creatures of habits and norms.

Authority of the office ...

Consider more closely the norm that the pastor is the congregation's official leader. While the image of the "Herr Pastor" may be a relic of immigrant days, vestiges remain. Lay people respect the clergy's education, and invite and expect strong clergy leadership. They will continue to hold the pastoral office in high regard, even when they are unhappy with those holding that office in their congregation.

Laity both honor and burden clergy with their pastoral expectations. Their first expectation is for good preaching and worship leadership. Active members value their congregation's worship life. It is one of the reasons they keep coming. They may tolerate pastors who are not strong administrators by offering their own organizational gifts, but they can't do the same for pastors who are not well prepared for, and effective in, worship. They listen each Sunday for sermons that will give clarity, hope and comfort.

Lay people expect their pastors to have the right words and special gifts to win prospective members, also. When new people come to church, lay members may offer words of welcome, but it is the pastor — trained in scripture and evangelism — who will bring those visitors into membership.

No wonder that laity also expect clergy to articulate a vision for congregational mission, and to set directions and goals. Even within churches actively engaging in strategic planning, many lay leaders will defer to the pastor's views. That may be out of respect or habit. Sometimes lay people find it easier to let pastors do it —isn't it their job? — and then criticize them later. But much of the time it is out of respect. Pastors enter congregations with high expectations awaiting them, but usually with the great respect and patience, laity will work with and support their pastors.

In effect, the pastor has the leading role, with lay members giving some leadership support and actively participating in congregational programs. Most congregations have definite ideas about what their pastors are to do, and how they are to allot their time. Some have written descriptions approved by church leaders. Few congregations ever discuss the expectations they have for lay members. Only the pastor carries stated, written leadership responsibility.

The role of members ...

This does not mean, however, that pastors have free rein to take their congregations in any direction they choose. Lay leaders set some boundaries. They may not articulate their views about what the church should be doing, but they make it clear what the church should not be doing. These leaders are guardians of a general model of the church that has evolved over the years. New pastors may "push the envelope" of that image somewhat, but they may not radically change the model. At least, they may not do so without dealing with the consequences.

Laity know that they are expected to give some time and money to the church. Beyond that, they often define their roles in connection with the pastor's role. The pastor is the worship leader, but should not have all the responsibility. While lay members and their pastors agree that members are to worship regularly, they may differ on how often "regularly" is. Choir, ushers, lectors and communion assistants play a helping role. The pastor may be in charge of planning programs, but laity share the committee work and lead programs when asked.

Thus, when it comes to sharing lay and clergy perspectives, congregations will have to work around the usual settings wherein pastors present views while lay leaders set limits, and other lay people give tacit approval. They will need to create settings in which all members are free to talk and question, are even encouraged to do so repeatedly. Churches will have to give permission to both pastors and laity to think beyond current boundaries, and then speak their minds.

The pressure of assumed purpose

Besides stated *role* expectations for clergy, and unstated ones for laity, congregations place *purpose* expectations on themselves. Purpose expectations are related to their program and services rendered, and their size and status in the community. Some churches summarize their purposes with measurable goals in mission statements. Depending on how widely these purposes are owned by church leaders, they exert a certain kind of pressure. Other congregations work on tradition and ongoing activities, rarely articulating or discussing their expectations. That generates a different kind of pressure.

The expectations congregations have for themselves add to the internal pressures to achieve that clergy bring to their work. Creative, capable pastors grow frustrated as they try to bring more members more frequently into worship and other congregational activities. Even pastors of thriving congregations push themselves toward larger goals. The demands, both internal and external, continue to grow.

Committed lay members add one more activity to their church time by spending one less evening elsewhere. Some spend one or two evenings a week at church. They perform three or four tasks on Sunday morning. Eventually, some experience "burn out", and new leaders are recruited to outline revised strategies to reach the same goals. The desire to make things work pushes their efforts. With mixed results, the cycle begins again.

Pressure increases on both pastors and lay members to make the congregation function as they expect it should, and as they assume others do, too. Sometimes there are resources to increase the professional staff, and the pressure can be managed. Sometimes congregations are situated in places that attract people interested in joining the church; but at other times and in other places, maintaining the congregation and avoiding membership decline dominates the efforts of both pastors and lay leaders. When they cannot meet ingrained expectations, the tension really builds.

Clergy and laity, devoted to the church, try to make their congregations live up to the images in their minds' eyes. They work hard. But when do they step back to discuss *why* they do the things that congregations do? When do they look outside to consider the places in which people work, or the pressures with which they live? Imagine what might happen if they paused to consider how their plans fit the mission God gives to the church. Pressures could be handled differently if congregations would habitually cultivate dialogue.

The habit of dialogue

Little wonder the idea of sharing perspectives is not very popular! It makes people tense, threatens the status of congregational leaders, and adds one more pressure to an already long list. What I've described thus far in this chapter could be used as a set or reasons why congregations are stuck in place. Changing habits is awkward. It takes work, persistence and some new skills. In this case, I firmly believe that creating a new habit of dialogue will be worth the effort. If you accept the notion that tension might be useful, and that the opinions of all congregation members have value, dialogue is a habit to consider.

Dialogue is different from discussion. Discussions are the conversations that occur among congregational leaders who are trying to solve problems or come to decisions. Their exchanges are aimed at reasoning out situations, arguing pros and cons, weighing options, making choices and planning actions. Churches are familiar with the habit of discussion.

Dialogue is an exchange of ideas that does not have to result in any choices or actions. It is sharing opinions without having to weigh or defend their merit. Sometimes, church members experience dialogue in small groups or Bible studies, but it is not a habit widely used in congregational meetings. Dialogue is underway when people:

- hear each other out, trying to see familiar things from the others' viewpoints.
- do not attempt to sway, change or belittle other viewpoints.
- treat each other as peers, not classifying some as more powerful than others.
- pay attention to what is important to others — what they need or fear losing.

Untying the strings of old habits ...

Set aside expectations of purpose and role

Congregations that wish to nurture a climate for dialogue begin by *temporarily* setting aside existing purpose and role expectations. This does not mean giving up familiar ideas. Rather, it means looking at existing expectations objectively, without becoming defensive or rushing to judgment.

Churches can start this process by recognizing that neither of the two perspectives outlined in Chapter 1 is better or truer than the other. Laity and clergy are not to be pitted against each other; their views are just different. It's as simple as the fact that the pastors' circumstances and daily responsibilities are not the same as those of lay people. Therefore, it's not a matter of trying to improve or change anyone's perspective, but of trying to understand, respect and build on the differences. Dialogue is more likely to happen when the climate is open and neutral, when it is safe to say anything.

Create places and times to foster dialogue

The second step is to create places and times to foster dialogue. Council and committee meetings are not good settings for that. They have established patterns for making plans and coming to decisions. Members would be frustrated by introducing a style that shows no immediate results. A leader retreat weekend might be a possibility, but limiting it to leaders would limit the shared perspectives.

Mini-retreats for members might work, carved out of Sunday afternoons or evenings and including a simple meal. Cottage meetings might work, or Wednesday evenings during Lent. What I'm looking for are times when members can get together fairly effortlessly. These would be times separate from established planning or decision-making meetings. They might be held at church, member homes, public places or lakeside cabins.

There could be impromptu times, also, with people lingering after meetings or programs. They could become a fellowship hour feature. The keys are informality and openness – anyone can join the conversation.

Ask for opinions; thank people for sharing

In congregations that want to share perspectives, people find ways to demonstrate acceptance of each other's viewpoints. Pastors and lay leaders ask many people for opinions, and thank them for sharing. They keep doing this until they notice that even average pew sitters are picking up the habit. It's called modeling behavior. Start with yourself and show others how to do it.

Imagine a dialogue occurring in the midst of a traditional Bible class. The teacher asks a question, resists giving an answer that breaks the silence, then, instead of commenting on the first answer, encourages others to add their views. The teacher lets the dialogue play itself out without wrapping it up or giving a right answer – just a "thank-you" for sharing thought-provoking opinions.

If congregations really want to explore perspectives, they will need more time than that afforded in a Bible class. Special times, places and open invitations become important. These gatherings have a focus but not an agenda. Their style is a relaxed, reflective exploration of the topic, with no lectures and no majority votes. Basic questions may form the topics:

Church

- How do you see the church?
- What place does it have in your everyday life?
- What are your hopes for our congregation?
- What do you expect of the pastor?
- What can the pastor expect from members?

Daily Life

- What is your daily work like? What do you do?
- What are the issues facing you, your co-workers and neighbors?
- How can the church help or support you when you are at work, school, home or in the community?

Mission

- What do you imagine God expects the church to be and do?
- How does our church carry the Gospel into the world?
- What might God be asking of us in our particular situation?

World

- What are the big issues that really concern you?
- What does scripture say about these issues?
- What parts of our community are in need of God's love?

To criticize or not ...

Listen uncritically

The next step is more difficult. Everyone, especially leaders, will have to work on their ability to welcome views others offer. They will learn to listen carefully, ask clarifying questions and check on word meanings *before* stating their own views. This means accepting the speaker's experiences and perspectives without criticism.

Re-think own views

At the same time, people learn to think more critically about their own perspectives. They ask themselves some questions. What has shaped their own views? What keeps them holding on to them so tightly? They grow in understanding when they look at their own perspectives critically while withholding judgment on the views others express.

Learning to see things from other points of view is not easy. People are more used to operating automatically on their own assumptions while challenging others. But if church leaders truly wish to explore other perspectives, the only ones they may rightfully criticize are their own. They will need to model this behavior so others will feel free to share minority opinions. They will need to keep these informal gatherings going until dialogue becomes a part of the rhythm of parish life.

With benefits ...

As leaders develop ability to receive the viewpoints of others uncritically, and to be more thoughtful about their own views, something interesting happens. Their image of church begins to change. They notice some things for the first time because someone else points out things that will stick in their minds.

Sharing perspectives *does* not mean changing perspectives to suit others. It does mean learning to evaluate congregational life in concert with people from other perspectives, *in order* to make good decisions together for the gathered community. That is much different than leaders making decisions for the church in private, based solely on personal views.

The tension between perspectives becomes beneficial when it is explored by peers who are trying to understand each other. Then it can build relationships rather than threaten them. People like it when others are willing to hear them out. They open up when they are not ridiculed for perceiving things differently. Shared information may lead to new ideas. An open, accepting climate may generate new energy. It could unearth some creative, innovative ways to strengthen congregations – and the will to try them.

End Notes

1   Gibson, William. *The Miracle Worker.* Bantam Books. 1959, 1960. Tamarack Productions, Ltd.

Chapter 3

Seek a clearer vision

"How could we do things differently inside to better carry God's love *outside*?" My third answer is perhaps the most important: *by seeking out God's perspective – together.*

The real value in sharing perspectives comes when our talk moves beyond how to improve things at church to conversation about God's will for the church. It comes when we take existing congregational goals and ask how they serve God's mission in this time and place. Search scripture, foster long conversations and frequent prayer within the congregation; then break away from the preoccupation of improving things on the inside. Step outside to see what God is doing – or wants done – in the world.

This experience may explain what I mean.

Which comes first? "Why?" or "How?"

Recently, I led a congregation council retreat. The council wanted to update its five-year plan which contained sections on worship, education, property, etc. At the retreat, I encouraged them to describe the results they wanted before they decided on steps to take. Why did they want to do the things the plan listed? What were they striving for in each part of congregational life? What qualities would define worship? What were the goals behind the education plan? What values would inform property decisions? How did any of this connect with the mission of the church?

These questions puzzled some council members, and I suspect they thought they were pointless. Surely, everyone knew the answers. But if the answers were really obvious, we would not have had such a hard time putting those supposedly common hopes into words. This was not the way these council members were used to talking together. They were more comfortable dealing with practical matters and making lists of things to

*do, such as training assisting ministers, changing the schedule for Sunday
school, remodeling the kitchen, etc.*

Have you had similar experiences? Does the worship committee discuss the needs members bring to worship, or the role of worship in
preparing members for the coming week? Does it express concern that
the way worship is conducted reflects the mission of the church? Or does
it spend its time setting schedules, assigning responsibilities, and debat-
ing about choir robes and hymn selection?

Putting mission into words

I find leaders spend much more time on keeping congregational life
going than on considering why their church does what it does, or how
that serves God's mission. Their perception about the church's business
is a legacy of experiencing how the church has operated for generations.
Therefore, instead of starting with the basic questions of "Why?" and
"What?", they jump to the third or fourth question, "How?", and move to
plan the next year's budget. Too often, church leaders assume that congregations should operate today as churches did when they were children.

Expectations of mission ...

When I ask congregational leaders how well they are fulfilling their
mission, the first subjects they usually mention are growth or attracting
new members. They talk about such things as welcoming
visitors and helping them find their way through
Sunday worship bulletins and hymnals. Eventually, talk turns to improving the educational program, keeping teenagers and young
adults involved, and carrying out social ministry activities in the community. When
someone mentions the condition of the building
and grounds, the conversation turns to finances.

Repeatedly, the discussion will turn to involving more people in doing
the congregation's work. Some complain that people who are doing all
the work now are the same ones who were doing it 10 years ago. Others
have elaborate systems for integrating new members. Most are concerned
about how to encourage interaction between new and longtime members.

Most of these conversations about mission center on who comes to church and how often, and what they do when they are there. Occasionally comments allude to service in the community and world, and to the time or financial support given to outside causes. Although they look at their congregations from different perspectives, both laity and clergy focus their expectations *inside*. They think about tangible, measurable, practical illustrations of mission as it happens within the gathered community of believers.

Would that be true in the congregations you know? Read their mission statements. How much of their mission is directed *inside*? How much sends them *outside*?

Getting to "Why?" ...

I'm not surprised that pastors and lay members think first of the practical matters of program and property. Their congregations probably are more welcoming, interesting places because of those efforts. But if that is as far as their thinking goes, they have not given God much room to challenge their perceptions of the church's mission. They are still trying to make congregations work using a decades-old model. Conversations need to go deeper — from tangibles to intangibles, from things they can do together to what God has called them to be, together and apart. That is the beginning of a changed-model congregation.

A case in point: Last year, my congregation set up a task force to improve Sunday school. As a result, we've instituted a number of practical things. Parents and other adults interact with children each Sunday. "Fourth-Sunday" projects alter the routine, producing sanctuary banners, treats for neighbors, food bank donations and gifts for the newly-baptized. We've provided Sunday school and worship connections in order for children to be active worship participants. These are good things.

What we have *not* done is to ask each other why Christian education is important, or how it fits into the mission God gives to the church. We've just tried to "fix" Sunday school so that it will be more attractive. Improving Sunday school is easier than finding words to define goals for nurturing members in their faith.

I'm not criticizing what the task force has been doing. I've been a willing, supportive group member. I'm simply using our experience to distinguish between doing practical, tangible things to improve church as we know it, and thinking about what God might want church to become in this time and place.

As the task force evolves, I hope we will talk about the intangibles. I hope we'll begin dialogues with adults who have not participated in Christian education for decades, and with parents who send children but won't come with them. What do they need to nourish their faith at this time in life? What are their hopes for our children? I'd like us to think about approaches other than Sunday school that might attract older youth — especially boys — who are reluctant to participate on Sunday mornings. Those are issues that are larger than "fixing" Sunday school!

When churchgoing insiders are able to move from tangibles to intangibles, they are ready to consider what God might have to say about the way they are being the church. That's different from simply pooling ideas or improving upon past practice. It moves people to a different level of sharing perspectives. They start by expressing what they know and want, then stretch to consider how that compares to what God might expect.

Common words, blurred vision ...

Recall my example at the beginning of Chapter 1. Two artists were painting a picture of the same tangible subject – a museum — with brushes. Now, I'm talking about drawing an intangible subject – the church in mission – with words. The phrase I used earlier was, "describing the church with my mind's eye." When churchgoers try to describe intangibles they see in their mind's eye, they may use a common vocabulary. To those listening, however, the words they speak may not have their intended meaning. People nod agreement, thinking they understand each other, when, in fact, words often convey slightly different mental images.

I once tried to demonstrate this by asking a group if an image came to their minds when I said "little white New England church with a steeple." They all nodded, so I gave everyone paper and pencil and asked them to draw that church. When they shared their drawings, each could be recognized as a New England church; yet, every picture was different.

Had I transferred those drawings to transparencies and stacked them on an overhead projector, they would have produced a very blurry picture. I believe churches operate today with a blurry vision of the church's mission, even when they begin to put it into words. Our common language lulls us into believing we understand and agree with each other, without taking time to clarify and test meanings. Developing a clear vision takes many words — tested, re-explained, applied to real situations and listened to carefully. It is an ongoing process, not a once-and-done chore.

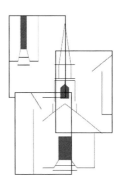

Inviting God's Perspective

I made a significant omission when I referred to prevailing views in Chapter 2, p. 28. I did not include the Word of God or the authority of scripture as factors in making decisions. In truth, I don't believe God's view is often sought out when congregations gather. I know that congregations pray for God's guidance, and councils may conduct Bible studies or authorize a series of cottage meetings on mission. But how many congregations have on-going dialogues about the purpose of the church, or engage in extended scripture study when dealing with specific issues? How many practice a daily prayer discipline for a month before making important decisions?

Most congregations' vision of mission is based primarily on memory and tradition. Churches behave as all institutions. Shaped by their corporate cultures, they conserve what has worked and been member pleasing. It is hard to change institutions that are not facing life-threatening crises.

But congregations are constituted as no other institution. They exist to serve God's will. Before churches willingly change their dependence on a decades-old model of congregational life, they must change the way they see the church in their mind's eye. That means allowing God's Spirit to become the prevailing voice in their discussions.

Reading scripture ...

One way to invite God's voice into church conversations is to make a practice of applying God's Word to situations congregations face. But isn't that what sermons do week after week? I don't think so. First of all, sermons are monologues, not dialogues. I'm looking for ways that Christians who come from different perspectives can put into words what they believe to be God's perspective. I want them to have opportunities to test their ideas with each other and find new insights.

Secondly, I believe sermons exemplify the church's habit of starting with scripture and then casting about for current situations to which the passage speaks. That is a good, important thing to do.

Scripture • Illustration • What God might be saying

In this instance, I want to reverse the sequence by suggesting that congregations – not just their preachers – become skillful at first naming issues or decisions facing them, and then search scripture for enlightenment. Start by articulating problems and opportunities from varied perspectives. When the issue — with its pros and cons — is clear to the congregation, go to scripture. Weave periods of prayer and times for reflection into the process. The practice I want to turn into a church habit is to search scripture for guidance on *already identified* congregational life concerns. If members learn to use the Bible this way at church, they are more likely to make it a practice when facing personal concerns in other places.

Current issue • Scripture • What God might be saying

Whenever I think about applying God's Word to congregational life, I remember what biblical scholar Walter Brueggemann says in his book *The Land*. Brueggemann explores the symbolic importance of land to Israel throughout the Old Testament. He recalls the period of history when the tribes were not content to be ruled by God through the judges, but demanded a king. They wanted their land to be governed like the nations surrounding them. However, God expected Israel's ruler, unlike the neighboring kings, to devote himself to study. Brueggemann describes the role of the king this way.

> *The central activity of the king is to read the Torah, that is, the primary function of the king is to keep management focused on the central memory and vision of Israel.*[2]

The king might spend time in everyday, practical activities such as leading warriors into battle, settling internal disputes, establishing laws, making treaties or stockpiling grain. But the crucial task always before him was to see that Israel did those activities in ways that kept it on track, true to its purpose.

The king was to remind Israelites of the exodus, the wilderness and settlement in Canaan —things God had done for them in the past. The king was to build a vision of the future by pointing to the covenant God made with them — promising to bless Israel so that they might be a blessing. The role of the king was to continually build the connection between the life issues Israel was facing and the Torah (God's law.)

I like the notion of pastors probing scripture to find guidance for the "management" issues facing the church. But I don't believe Brueggemann was recommending a contemporary leadership style. Rather, I think he was describing the importance of keeping the people of God focused on God's purpose for them. That remains important today. Clergy and laity are responsible together to see that this happens. The church is the Body of Christ, created to carry out God's plans. Keeping God's word front and center reminds the church that it has a mission, also.

The portion of the Brueggemann quote that I appreciate most comes at the end. The words give equal importance to memory and vision. Congregations that spend their time talking about practical matters are focused on memory. They shape their future life by remembering the past. Reading scripture would help them recall how the church was established. It would add a deeper dimension to their personal memories.

More importantly, reading scripture would help them develop a vision for the future, one that is informed by the past but not restricted by it. Reading scripture would create balance between memory and vision. A central vision of life lived in covenant with God gives permission to change and encourages moving in new directions. A clear, understood vision allows the church to manage well its choices and actions. The force of that vision could help congregations come unstuck. It would make all the difference in their world.

Congregations need to learn to read the Bible together. Their pastors play a significant role in doing this as instructors and interpreters. (See suggestions in Chapters 5 and 7.) But the rest of the members need to be vocal students as well. It is their dialogue that will develop clear meanings once they have probed, questioned, used various examples and tried different combinations of words.

Reading the world ...

Churches need to look for God's perspective outside the church, also. They need to learn to search the world as well as the Bible. God creates and still loves the world. Wherever there is human need, whenever there is injustice or violence, God is calling the church to attention and action.

If this were a just, merciful society, congregations wouldn't need to spend much energy thinking about the church in the world. Or about changes they might make inside the church to better take God's love outside. But the 21st Century world is not yet noted for justice or mercy.

The American way of life at the beginning of the 21st Century is pluralistic. There are multiple American ways of life now for Christians and non-Christians. Some do not include the every-Sunday churchgoing that typified my childhood. By necessity or choice, Sunday is the day for chores, shopping, school sports and leisure activities. For many people living around me, it is a workday.

Older church members grew up when mission meant evangelism in foreign countries where people had not heard of Christ. Now mission also means evangelism in North America, because people here have not heard of Christ.

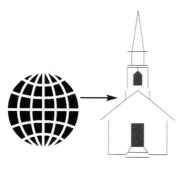

By necessity and by choice, churchgoers are not having as many children as their grandparents. Many children today do not know the Bible stories I was taught year after year in Sunday school. They don't know the story of Joseph's coat, Samson's long hair, or the boy's lunch of bread and fish. They haven't been introduced to Mary, Martha and Lazarus. They are not able to find comfort in Lot's laments, or inspiration in Isaiah's visions.

Many who live outside the church haven't a clue about the Bible or life lived with the Lord. They are hassled single parents who've never been inside a church, and don't know how God's grace can sustain them day after a difficult day. They are successful entrepreneurs who believe they can do anything and need no one. They are children in day care centers who know Christmas only as a holiday for receiving gifts. How do they hear the stories of Jesus if they aren't coming to church?

Technology, making life automated and anonymous, tends to diminish the unique value of each person. The drive for success puts emphasis on numbers, not individuals. Family structures and social circles are different today. How does the church of my childhood fit life as people live it now? How much should the church change to accommodate changes in daily life and life styles? One answer sounds as though it compromises absolutes. Another seems to hang some foolish millstones around the necks of new generations.

Consider the changes in societal values over the last four decades. I've lived through the 60s with "hippie" children who didn't buy into their parents values. That's the same decade the civil rights movement finally caught the nation's attention. It caught the church's attention, too, especially in older neighborhoods experiencing ethnic or economic change. Whether congregations stayed or took flight, they were never the same again. Congregations are still wrestling with differences in belief and practice when it comes to accepting outsiders who are of different class, race or lifestyles. Churches may be in a better place now than they were in my segregated, closeted childhood neighborhood, but they don't live in an easier place.

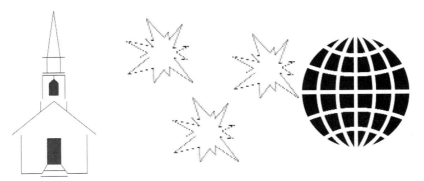

The Vietnam War diverted attention from our nation's civil rights struggles. Church leaders and their children were sorely divided on the rightness of this conflict. Political dissent grew and respect for government declined. Younger generations are not as likely as I was to follow in their parents' footsteps. Global issues have changed local worlds. Yet churches continue to work on old, taken-for-granted assumptions about God's mission.

The Word of God has something to say about the church's mission beyond church property lines. It calls congregations to pay attention to the world outside, and drives them back to reading scripture. What has God done in the past? How does God ask the church to be a blessing in the world in future times? The section titled *Re-balancing the Vision of Mission*, in Chapter 6, suggests some ways to read the world.

New urgencies ...

You can make your own lists that count the ways the world is changing. So much happens so quickly in this instant information age that it tends to numb me. I wonder if it numbs congregations, too, making them less tolerant of external pressures, and more determined to stick with unspoken assumptions about being the church. Yet, here congregations stand — in the midst of a fast-changing world. God looks for them to be a blessing there. At some point congregations need to overcome inertia and re-think the church's mission.

A new sense of urgency might get them started. An Episcopal rector in one of Gail Godwin's novels puts it this way:

> *Don't you think we all store much of our knowledge on back shelves, until something ... some new urgency ... compels us to go back and reexamine it? .... Maybe that's how changes in people have to start ... with something close to us.... Something we can accept emotionally.*[3]

I like this because it suggests that I need to be emotionally ready to reexamine knowledge. It's not just a matter of intellect or logic. I will re-examine what I already know when something stirs feelings in me. I don't equate "accept emotionally" with feeling good and comfortable; that doesn't prompt change. I believe Godwin's term applies more to realizing that something touching my life is different, though I haven't been willing to admit it. Now I see it for what it is. Accepting emotionally is getting past denial. That's when change can begin. That's when I go back to examine what I know, and to re-think my assumptions.

I believe changes in society should prompt us church-goers to search our back-shelf knowledge. We've watched church attendance decline – including participation by many of our own Sunday-school-raised offspring. That stirs my emotions! We've seen media and special interest groups define values that set Christians at odds with neighbors and co-workers. Do you get upset, as I do, over the stories of youth shooting other youth because they feel that no one understands them? Or about parents so stressed and preoccupied that they leave their babies strapped into car seats in overheating vehicles? Things close to us are not what they used to be. It's time to name them, and to ask God what they tell us about the church's mission in this time and place.

What might happen if congregation members began to name the worldly issues that touch them emotionally? Could that prompt them to re-examine their back-shelf information about being the church? If they did, if they read scripture, God's spirit could show them ways to change the church inside in order to bring more love to God's world *outside*.

End Notes

2   Brueggemann, Walter. *The Land*. Fortress Press, Philadelphia. 1977. p.77

3   Godwin, Gail. *Evensong*. Ballantine Publishing Group, Random House, Inc., NY. 1999. p.18

2nd idea:
Re-think ideas long taken for granted

Chapter 4

Shake out assumptions

Posing the question "How could we do things differently *inside* to better carry God's love *outside*?" brings to mind images of specific things we do when we go to church. We remember real people, special events and moments of joy or sorrow shared within our congregations. Why would we want to do things differently at church?

Why? We are prompted to do things differently when recent experiences no longer fit comfortably into old practices. New urgencies cause us to re-examine patterns and ideas long taken-for-granted. Why? We look to the Bible for guidance, and find new meanings in familiar passages. Someone asks a question, and it disturbs us because our quick answers don't sound so convincing to our own ears. When we are ready to look at the "back shelf knowledge" Gail Godwin's rector talks about, we are becoming ready to do church things differently. In this chapter my answer to the book's basic question is: *by re-considering assumptions about "church" and "mission" long taken-for-granted.* I liken these assumptions to old clothes stored in a cedar chest.

The Cedar Chest

It happened every August in my childhood home, usually on one of the hottest days. Mother would take me upstairs, open the cedar chest and shake out old skirts and dresses packed inside. Some were clothes I had worn the previous year. Most were my older sister's castoff school clothes. Mother would hold up one item of clothing after the other. Did it fit across the shoulders? Was the waist too long? Then I would try them on.

There was no air-conditioning. The wool was scratchy. I had to stand still and keep my shoulders straight. Mother tucked and pinned, trying to make old clothes fit. Sometimes it worked pretty well. But as I grew older,

I became aware that, despite her skilled needlework, my sister's clothes still looked like hand-me-downs. They did not suit me. They did not reflect current styles. I wanted new clothes.

Assumptions are something like old clothes. They were first worn because they fit and were in style. We continued to wear them if they were durable and comfortable. We even wore our favorite clothes when the fit was not so good by "letting out" the waistband. Some favorite clothes may still hang in the back of our closets.

So it is with assumptions. Ideas we found comfortable long ago are tucked away in our minds. We haven't thought about them in years. Church goers have stored away a lot of assumptions about the church and its mission since their childhood. Some have been passed along from one generation to another.

In this chapter we'll look at four familiar assumptions about church and mission that have guided leaders for generations. We'll unpack them, shake them out, hold them away from us awhile and see how they look now. We'll examine them, not to prove them wrong, for they have been good, well-used ideas. But we need to see how well they fit today's circumstances.

Do the assumptions still ring true?

Or do they look different
when we view them from another angle?

I. Develop strong, growing congregations

Congregations should grow in numbers and strength. Perhaps no other assumption is more basic to American church life. Leaders take it for granted. But if I were to ask "Why?" someone might explain further: *The greater the number of church members, the wider the knowledge of the Gospel in our community.*

This kind of reasoning is based on the notion that the church is the means for learning about God's love. Images of Sunday school classes and preaching pastors come to mind. Christians take heart that the Gospel is being spread to people living around them when new members join their congregations. The more churchgoing members, the more people who are becoming Jesus' disciples.

So leaders work hard to develop strong, growing congregations. Countless pastors, lay people and regional and national church staff have designed programs and conducted training events to help congregations flourish. Developing strong, growing congregations has been the main way to proclaim the Gospel in North America. Think about that, and consider how this assumption has been re-enforced in practice.

The 1st Assumption: Congregations should grow in numbers and strength.

Look at the numbers …

Denominational offices gather congregational statistics annually to check on numbers, dollars, programs and other aspects of congregational life. If churches are interested in having strong, growing congregations, these are important measurements. They may be compared to my doctor checking my vital signs when I go for a physical exam. Numbers provide indicators regarding my health. Over time, they show patterns which provide further clues to my well-being.

That is also true for church statistics. Statistics identify areas where congregations are gaining or losing members. They help plan where new congregations might be started, how congregational giving is keeping up with inflation, and how much money congregations are sharing benevolently. That information is used to predict, among other things, how many social ministry services can be supported with benevolence funds. By reading the numbers year after year, national church leaders have learned much about what kind of people join congregations, the frequency with which they worship, the programs in which they are active, and the causes to which they devote their benevolence dollars.

But how is statistic-gathering perceived?

For some congregational leaders, annual report forms feel like a test on which they will be graded. Statistics set out categories that are perceived as measures of success. The reports become a way for the denomination to appraise performance and pass judgment. Why is per capita giving up in this congregation, but not in the one across town? Which pastors are increasing worship attendance by drawing in more church-going members?

Because statistics are limited to measurable categories, other marks of success go unrecorded. Congregations can report numbers of Sunday school members, but have no way to tell how much more confidence students have in their ability to pray aloud. They can report how many dollars are placed in the offering plate, but have no way to share how families are changing their life styles as part of their stewardship. Some congregations that are just "holding their own" numerically in declining communities are probably more vital than other congregations growing at a rate slower than the booming communities around them. But which congregations are seen as most successful? Numbers count.

Statistics, meant to track trends, become a means of judgment. The annual request for measurable facts becomes an implied goal. What do denominations want to know about congregations? How big do they have to be to be considered viable? Truth be told, numbers become one means of judgment in providing financial aid and in deciding what kind of pastoral services can be expected in small congregations. They are more than neutral measurements. They re-enforce the notion that the church wants bigger congregations with more financial resources.

Consider the message to clergy ...

Pastors rely on worship attendance records because they are one of the few ways to take the 'pulse" of the congregation or judge their own effectiveness. If congregations functioned as most corporations do, pastors would receive an annual performance appraisal from their supervisors. But congregations operate differently. The pastor is the paid executive officer who is supervised by an elected group of volunteers. Too often those elected boards or councils are not well equipped to supervise, or to give pastors candid feedback on a regular basis. Without some regular process of goal setting and evaluation, pastors rely on numbers to judge how well their leadership is received.

A letter published recently in one denomination's professional journal puts the issue clearly. The writer was responding to an article about the need for pastoral presence when members are in crisis.

....As time marches on, I discover that such time spent does not easily translate into money in the offering tray nor attendance at church. Increasingly, this becomes the implicit (if not explicit) measuring rod of pastoral performance.

Time spent in the hospital or nursing home does not easily translate into church growth in a current atmosphere which views numbers as a priority (that is, dollars and attendance).

....The fact is that pastoral performance is becoming more and more measured by numerical results, time spent in committee meetings, and the number of worship services offered (to diverse seekers and people who want to sleep in on Sunday).[4]

It's after they graduate from seminary that clergy often absorb the assumption that congregations are to be growing in numbers and strength. As students, more emphasis was placed on their abilities as worship leaders, preachers, scholars, teachers and pastoral counselors. Congregations want pastors with these capabilities, of course. But they also want assurance that the pastor will make the congregation better and (at least a little) bigger than it has been.

Being the leader of a strong, growing congregation seems to be the secret to success. Not only do congregational leaders expect this, so do denominational leaders. Pastors see that their colleagues with records of "growing" one congregation often move on to more promising congregations. The financial reality is that the better paying positions are in larger congregations. Clergy paying off student loan debts, or supporting growing families, can't ignore that fact. Whatever else they hoped to achieve as pastors, their personal finances press them to make "more members" a goal.

Self-expectations press them, also. Pastors, wanting their congregations to be strong growing ones, try to develop them in many ways. They work harder on sermons, contemporary worship services, evangelism programs and social activities that will attract people. And the task stays difficult. Certainly, there are stories about really big, successful congregations. But those examples are far and few between. In fact, they add to the pressure. What else should pastors of typical congregations be doing? Too many bear a personal burden for not being able to elicit a greater response from more members.

Think of the members ...

Congregations are gathered communities of specific people in real places. Sustaining these congregations becomes very personal to long-time members who have loved a particular church and its ways since they were children. They have fond memories of being in Christmas pageants in the same church nave where their children's Christmas plays are staged. They've been sitting in the same pew for years. In some cases, their ancestors are buried in the church cemetery. The processional cross was given as a memorial to their parents. Church for them is strongly associated with a particular building and what happens there.

People who have moved from one congregation to another can demonstrate these same strong feelings. Even new congregations need to deal with tradition. Many charter members remember customs practiced in their childhood churches. Congregations today have been shaped by norms and habits that made churches strong and growing 20, 40 or 50 years ago. Those memories define continuing expectations for the church in the future.

Because members value their current experience in a particular congregation, they want it to continue for themselves and for those they love. They want new church-going members to join who will share their expectations and burdens. How many years should the same members need to teach Sunday school or keep the choir going? When will other people pitch in to prepare the Easter breakfast or stewardship dinner?

Longtime members worry when attendance declines or there is a budget deficit. They rejoice when couples with young children visit. They want a congregation strong enough to carry on the good things it has been doing. They look to the pastor to keep them headed in that direction.

Shaking out the first assumption ...

Congregations should be growing in numbers and strength. I began with this simple assumption. *The greater the number of church members, the wider the knowledge of the Gospel in our community.* Now, look at it from a different angle.

There are two ideas behind this assumption. One is about the *number of members.* The other is about *knowledge of the Gospel.* Which one drives the other? Or should one drive the other? If there is truth in the paragraphs you've just read, *numbers* have become the driving force for knowledge. Growth seems to be the evidence of the spread of the Gospel.

What happens if *knowledge of the Gospel* becomes the driving force behind the assumption? That makes strong, growing congregations a supporting strategy. From this view, attention centers on the people who do not know Christ or are not secure in his love. How does the church – how do we – share the Gospel with people who live nearby, as well as with people who live half-a-world away? From this angle, recruiting new members and building up the institution become secondary and supportive to sharing God's love.

The Gospel mission of the church ...

What is God's mission for baptized Christians? Are they to build up the congregation, or deliver the Gospel? Matthew, Mark, Luke and John record that Jesus seems to have offered little guidance on how his followers were to organize themselves, though other New Testament books do report some organizational patterns that developed after the first Pentecost.

Jesus concentrated on spreading Good News. He drew crowds who wanted to hear his teachings and feel his healing touch. He told followers first to love God and then to love neighbors, strangers and enemies. He asked them to be light and yeast in the world, to seek justice, and to offer the downtrodden a cup of cold water. Jesus called disciples, taught them by word and example, and then sent them out to preach and heal. Matthew's Gospel ends with Christ giving the Great Commission to "Go to the people of all nations and make them my disciples." I believe the mission of the whole church – and all its congregations – is to love God, and to carry God's love into the world to people of all conditions, both near and far.

From my perspective, the church exists to praise God and enable its members to carry out God's intentions in the world — to be Gospel-carrying outsiders. It has always been the world God has been after. "For God so loved the world that he gave his only Son ..." The world is the object of God's saving action and loving grace. Somehow, whenever I muse on this, I'm reminded of the famous sign posted in the Clinton campaign offices in 1992. That sign read *It's the economy, stupid.* And I wonder if there should be a sign in every church office with a similar message. *It's the world, you white-washed sepulchers!* It's so simple. Everyone knows it. God did not send Jesus so that there might be large, successful churches. Christ walked this earth to show people life and love as God intended it.

"For God so loved the world ... "

Several years ago, I was working with teams of congregational leaders at an unusual retreat center high in the California redwoods. The center was designed for international government officials and institutional scholars. Interesting books and artifacts lined shelves in the common meeting room, and a huge relief map of the world dominated one wall. As the staff prepared for the seminar, we looked for a large wall space on which to hang some newsprint. There was a great spot next to the map, but the lighting was poor. One staff member found a ladder that reached the ceiling spotlight shining on the map. He intended to shift it to our newsprint and put it back on the map before we left. But the spotlight would not swivel; it was fixed in place. We could not take the spotlight off the world. *It's the world, you church-going members!*

Suppose a congregation had gathered funds for additional lighting. Should they be used to illuminate the stained glass windows so they would glow inside the church? Or should they be spent to spotlight areas outside, so the church could better see the community? A North Carolina pastor posed this kind of question in the congregation's newsletter, noting that the congregation already possessed the light of Christ inside the church so they were free to shine their light outward to the world. *It's the world, in need of Gospel-carrying outsiders!*

God will not let the church obscure the world or leave it in darkness. If congregations are to be true to Christ's Great Commission, they need to look beyond institutional walls to see God's world.

A means to the end …

To develop strong, growing congregations, we must be motivated by the driving need to take God's love into the world. That makes numbers a strategy, not a goal. Strong, growing congregations become a means to an end, not an end in themselves.

The Great Commission was not to build up the church, but to make disciples. The church developed as a means to that end. Disciples needed to gather to worship, tell faith stories and gain courage from each other. Their need to "congregate" turned into organized, institutional practices.

The 1st Assumption, re-viewed: Congregations should carry God's love into the world.

The church has evolved and changed over the centuries. In North America, it followed early settlers, supported immigrant populations and became a missionary outpost to Native Americans. Congregations have been a significant feature of community life, shaping "traditional" American morals and values and spreading the Gospel across the continent.

Because of its success, planting the church – congregation by congregation – has become the dominant strategy for spreading the Gospel. Church leaders have tried to expand the model with supportive strategies such as social services, but developing strong congregations remains front and center in institutional planning. It isn't often that other strategies or agencies that deliver God's love are considered.

With all that attention, it is no wonder that the strategy has been perceived at times as an end in itself. Certainly, it is easier to measure the elements of the strategy (numbers, programs, dollars) than to determine how widely the Gospel is known in the community. Training preachers and Sunday school teachers to proclaim the Gospel in church is easier than equipping lay people to carry the Gospel into their daily places. Church leaders work hard at that strategy, but will it accomplish the mission or simply preserve the institution?

Is developing strong congregations the best Christians can do? I began with this assumption: Congregations should grow in numbers and strength. The greater the number of church members, the wider the knowledge of the Gospel in our community. Having considered the old assumption from another angle, I might restate it: *Congregations should carry God's love into the world.*

In other words, congregations are *"com-missioning centers" – one of the means God uses to deliver the Gospel in particular places, in partnership with other groups, and through their members' daily discipleship.* They can grow in strength, and perhaps in numbers, as they focus energy on being Gospel-carriers.

II. Go to church

The basic assumption about strong, growing congregations is underlined by the supporting assumption that members should go to church regularly. It is an assumption that was drilled into me from childhood. *People who really believe the Gospel will express their faith by worshiping weekly and participating in other church activities.*

Disciples have been gathering to praise God and support each other since that first Easter. Christians go from their daily life settings to places where they can be with other believers and then return again to daily places. This coming and going is commonly referred to as the church gathered and scattered.

The 2nd Assumption:
Members should worship regularly.

For church-goers, it's hard to imagine life without regular times of gathering for worship. And hard to understand how others can identify themselves as Christian without connecting themselves to congregations.

Hope mingled with fear ...

Consider how the character of the gathered community has evolved. I have no difficulty imaging some of the motivation that must have drawn 1st Century Christians together. Joy and amazement would have overwhelmed Christ's followers as the news of his resurrection spread. They must have recounted their stories over and over, savoring the memories of their experiences and praising God. They would have been excited as they anticipated Christ's return and the coming of the God's Kingdom. Everything would be so different! No more problems, pain or grief. The gathered community was a place of celebration, eagerness and joy.

Those who had not been eyewitnesses would have wanted to hear the stories of Jesus, too. It must have been reassuring to hear again and again that all this really did happen. Those who had never met Jesus would have asked questions, trying to understand more about this man-God.

- **What was Jesus like?**
- **Where did he come from?**
- **How did you meet him?**
- **Did he actually heal that blind man?**
- **Will he take me into his kingdom – am I good enough?**

The gathered community was a place to learn and exchange information.

When Christ did not return as expected, other emotions must have surfaced. Some followers must have felt confusion, even betrayal.

- **Why had Jesus not returned?**
- **How were they supposed to live?**
- **Should they return to their old lives?**
- **What could they say to others about Jesus?**

The gathered community must have tried to puzzle out answers to their questions. They taught each other how to talk about their faith and to share it with others.

Some Christians were ridiculed, others persecuted. The initial excitement was tempered with fear. Their faith was tested from within and without. The gathered community became a place to share fears, find renewed strength, courage, help and healing.

Prosperity and property ...

Christians *found* places to gather in the church's first centuries: in homes, by rivers, in caves and other secluded spots. I suppose those places changed as need or opportunity dictated. Practices could be adapted to meet new situations. Christianity was still a movement and not yet an institution. The church was institutionalized when Christianity became the Roman Empire's official religion.

Then Christians *built* places to gather, since they no longer needed to gather in secret. They needed large places. Now there were both those who truly believed and those who were forcefully baptized. Anyone who has seen some of the old cathedrals of Europe knows that whole towns could be packed into the huge naves that dominate those buildings. And they were; it was the law.

Many European immigrants brought the image of those cathedrals with them to North America, along with their worship habits. They built new places of worship, though on a much smaller scale. Others brought their defiance of those same images and habits. They, too, built places of worship — usually modest and plain. Americans have built churches — from storefronts to large suburban campuses and simple country chapels — from coast to coast. The landscape is dotted with a wonderful variety of church buildings. They house believers with widely differing understandings and ways to practice their faith.

Ministry institutionalized ...

Overall, immigrant Christians functioned in a flexible manner while they were establishing their homes and livelihoods. As years passed and as they acquired more resources, settled Christians were able to expand responses to Christ's commands to spread the Word and be good Samaritans. When a strategy worked well, it became part of a regular routine; congregations institutionalized ministry activities.

For example, worshiping in a neighbor's home – with or without clergy – was replaced by worship led in separate church buildings by circuit-riding preachers. Family Bible reading was supplanted by sending children to Sunday school. Spontaneous efforts to care for those in need grew into orphanages, old folks' homes, hospitals and modern-day social ministry services. Congregations banded together in regional and national organizations to establish seminaries, provide financial support for foreign missionaries, and start new congregations across the American landscape. If immigrants left the institutional church behind when they left Europe, they quickly re-institutionalized it when they were settled in America.

Being an institution is neither positive nor negative. The way the institution supports God's mission, however, can enhance or deter that mission. "Institutionalize" is not a friendly term. While it describes structuring activities into a formal system, it sometimes is used to label practices that are rigidly stuck in place. Organizations tend to lose their flexibility, and do not deal with change quickly. One of the symptoms of resistance to change is the familiar phase repeated in church meetings, "But we've never done it that way before." The danger for the institutional church is that love of the church can overwhelm love of its Lord.

The church is a unique institution, but it is an institution, nonetheless. Some independent groups led by charismatic pastors might still qualify as "movements" – unless they have checking accounts! Any group that has a constitution, tax I.D. number, property, elected officials, employees, corporate culture and traditions is an institution. Most churches in North America are well-organized institutions with clearly-defined powers and firmly-established leaders.

The institutional nature of the church is evident in all its parts – congregations, schools, regional and denominational offices. Each part has personnel concerns, property maintenance issues, stated and unstated ways of doing things. Church-goers may not like to think of the business side of being a congregation, but it is real.

Institutions want to preserve themselves from generation to generation. Certainly, those who are part of the church want their influence to be felt for years to come. Good intentions are often frustrated by an organization that has lost flexibility. Buildings, employees, memorial chapels, cemeteries, constitutions and generations of the same family in power all establish patterns that discourage fresh thinking. First century

Christians were good at responding to new circumstances. American immigrant congregations were, too. But churches today are hampered by practices that were institutionalized in another era, for a world that no longer exists.

Shaking out the second assumption ...

Members should go to church regularly. Worshiping is an outgrowth of the long held assumption that *people who really believe the Gospel will express their faith by weekly worship and participating in other church activities.*

This fits nicely with the reasoning behind the first assumption. The way to tell who the believers are is to see who shows up at church. Institutions have members. Congregations track attendance and giving; that way they know who has heard and responded to the Gospel. From this view, going *inside* is the way Christians show commitment and express faith. Those who stay *outside* are either people who have not heard the Gospel, or do not consider it important for their lives. That draws a pretty sharp distinction between believers and nonbelievers.

Does this assumption really mean that being an active member of the church is all that God expects of believers? If so, it's not much. A couple of hours a week and a few dollars in the offering plate leaves the rest of the week free from obligation? Surely there is more to being Christian than going to church!

What about Christians who don't worship or participate in church activities regularly? What allowances does this assumption make for those whose work schedules or disabilities make participation in traditional church activities impossible? Think of all those who tell pollsters they believe in God. Or consider the grocery clerk I know whose pastor refused her Holy Communion because of something he thought she did. What about risk-taking members who have challenged tradition, or pushed social issues and have been rejected by their congregations?

In an article entitled "Church as a Community of Ex-centric People", J. Paul Rajashekar of Philadelphia Lutheran Seminary says:

> *...despite a decline in registered membership in the church, there are millions of people in Western societies who claim to be Christian, albeit*

"churchless Christians." Those inside the church have a tendency to belittle such "unchurched" and seek ways to "bring them in" when those outside do not feel the need to associate themselves with church communities. Those "churchless Christians" seem to be estranged and disillusioned with established churches and have sought alternative forms of community.[5]

Is church-going the only measure of faith? Is the church building the only place where Christians can worship and share the Gospel?

Members through baptism …

We church-goers become members of the church not because we attend regularly, but because we are baptized. Participation is a response, not a condition.

Baptism is a tender act, made powerful by God's claims and promises. The baptized person is received by God and promised the most amazing extended family. Think of having brothers and sisters around the world who will recognize you and help you wherever you go. A German family took me into their home sight-unseen because I was part of a church youth delegation. We prayed the Lord's Prayer together even though we could not understand each other's words. Chinese Christians made room for me on a crowded bench at the beginning of a worship service. We sang "Holy, Holy, Holy" to the same tune, but using different languages.

Christians are members of one family. That's quite a gift! We church-goers live our lives assured of our worth because we are important to our Creator. What love God gives us! As we are blessed and drawn into God's family, we also assume family responsibilities. We join the priesthood of all believers…

that we may proclaim the praise of God and bear his creative and redeeming Word to all the world.[6]

Church-goers are part of the company of believers who receive the Word and Sacraments, and who follow Christ's example by sharing the Good News, serving others and working for justice and peace in the world.

Notice that once again, the context is the world. Baptized Christians carry God's love into the world. Going to church is not enough. It is not the measure of faith, but a means of sustaining faith. It is one place to share the faith, but not the main place. That's still the world.

Variously gifted ...

All baptized Christians do not have the same gifts, but all are gifted. That's part of the wonder of God's creative power. Unique from birth and called in baptism, Christians have God's promise that they have particular gifts they need for ministries in the world and the church. Some gifts are obvious from childhood; others come as a surprise later in life. Our gifts include natural abilities, learned skills and experiences, opportunities, interests and ways of thinking.

The combination of gifts with which individuals are blessed, and their life circumstances, send them in different directions. Some, — such as pastors, lay professionals, musicians or administrators — take paths that lead to service in the institutional church. However, gifts and circumstances lead most baptized Christians in directions other than professional church work. They may be active in congregational ministries, but they use their gifts primarily outside the congregation.

Church-going insiders need to be reminded that what Christians do outside is important, too. Gifts exercised outside the church are as valuable as those offered inside. Christians who do their daily work competently and with integrity teach poor migrant workers to read, research case histories to release the wrongly-imprisoned, restore eyesight to those suffering from cataracts, and enact laws to protect children oppressed by unfair labor practices.

The 2nd Assumption, re-viewed: Members should be the church always.

Some lay members may not understand that the exercise of their gifts at work, home, school and in the community is ministry on Christ's behalf. It is a foreign idea to them.

DiAnne enters patient records into the computer system of a hospital in Charlotte, North Carolina. I met her several years ago when she was dumbfounded that someone in our seminar suggested that she ministered as she did her work. For her, "ministry" was the quiet Saturday time at church when she prepared the altar for communion; it was her visits to shut-ins to whom she could bring flowers and hugs. So she shook her head in doubt. Then someone asked "What might happen to the patients if you did not enter the data accurately?" Everyone in the room knew the answer. DiAnne still struggles with the idea that her anonymous record keeping is what God calls her to do. How does the church help her when she grew up thinking only religious, charitable activities qualify as ministry?

Pastor Alice attended the same seminar. She listened in amazement to the conversation with DiAnne. She had always assumed that lay people knew they were baptized ministers serving in God's world. Six months later, members of her congregation told their pastor that they had noticed a change in her preaching. She acknowledged this and wrote:

I notice a shift in my preaching away from preaching the Gospel as a work of art to be admired. The Gospel wears overalls and I try to preach the application and living out of the Gospel in daily life. I think members feel a new sense of personal mission. [The seminar] has washed the dust off this longstanding truth for them and for me.[7]

The longstanding truth of God's call is reaffirmed in each and every baptism. How does the church wash that truth clean so that all Christians hear God's call to them in particular and without doubt?

I began with this well-worn assumption: Members should worship regularly. *People who really believe the Gospel will express their faith by weekly worship and participating in other church activities.* I might rewrite the old assumption now by substituting another verb:

Members should *be* the church always.

Looking at the church from a different angle reveals that *people who are baptized will express their faith when they gather with other Christians, both inside the church and when they use their gifts to serve God in their daily places.*

III. Attract new members

Concern for growth prompts another assumption: Congregations should draw new people into membership. Somewhere along the way, church-goers concluded that *if unchurched people would just come into the church building, they would hear the Gospel, enjoy the fellowship and join the church.*

More people in church means more people know the Gospel. The place to learn about the Gospel is in church. The congregation's task is to find ways to keep members coming and to attract new people into their fellowship.

Choosing a congregation to join ...

I suppose evangelism programs designed to win new members really developed with the post World War II home building explosion. During a college year summer, I was part of a team that knocked on front doors on street after street of a new suburb, Monroeville, Pennsylvania. We distributed a brochure describing the new mission there and took names of those who would be interested in a follow-up visit. My memory is that nearly 100 people joined the congregation at the end of the summer. Rapid growth like this occurred in many places in the 50s and early 60s.

The 3rd Assumption:
Congregations should draw new people
into membership.

"Initial visits," like the ones we did, remain a basic part of current evangelism programs, but many other ingredients have been added. After my parish pastor husband retired, we visited several churches in our community to consider which one might become our new church home. When we worshiped in a congregation for the first time, we could predict that a visitor would stop by in the afternoon to drop off a box of cookies. Letters and brochures followed. Pastors called.

What I'm describing, of course, are standard elements of contemporary evangelism programs. In most congregations we visited, it was obvious that they had step-by-step strategies for responding to first-time worshippers. When someone new came through the door, they had a plan in place to try to draw them back again. Their goal was to win new members to the congregation.

If we just get them inside ...

Congregations that are interested in drawing new people to their churches often don't wait for people just to show up. They find potential new members in other ways. Mass mailings, tele-canvassing invitations, and ads on billboards and during radio broadcasts are designed to give the congregation visibility in the community. Some place floats in local parades; others sponsor booths at the fair. Many creative things are done to send the message that congregations are interesting, attractive places that are worth a visit.

A number of congregations offer events, programs and services that making a first visit to church easier for strangers. Strawberry festivals, ham dinners, pork barbecues – all kinds of foods are advertised, along with invitations for the public to share the meal. The same is true of choir concerts, organ recitals and Easter egg rolls. Congregations allow community groups and scout troops to use their facilities. The list could go on. Not that the goal of all these efforts is to produce new members. Some activities are simple continuations of longstanding traditions or commitments. Others occur because outsiders asked to use the building. The facilities themselves may lend to certain uses – a gym needed for the inter-church volleyball league, an acre of open ground that is perfect for a community garden, a church on a bus route making it well-suited for the community clothes closet.

As a result of public use of church property, however, most pastors and lay leaders hope that *some* new members will be identified. They believe that as outsiders become familiar with their congregations, they will be attracted to them.

Hear religious language ...

Part of the logic of this assumption is that the place where the Gospel is best heard is inside the church. So congregations need these strategies to bring the unchurched inside to tell them the Good News. Many current evangelism strategies depend on drawing outsiders in first.

The logic continues that, once newcomers arrive, the main responsibility for turning visitors into members rests with the pastor. Lay people have some role in welcoming newcomers, but it's the pastor's job to proclaim and teach the Word. Pastors are trained to spread the Gospel. So *their* sermons, *their* visits to prospects, *their* new-member instruction classes are key to winning new members. Active members may feel some obligation to invite outsiders to visit, but they see themselves as Gospel-hearers more than Gospel-carriers.

Faith stories and religious language are largely relegated to church. Many members work in places where sharing one's faith would be frowned upon; at least, that is their perception. Lay members may use religious language at home, but chances are that's about the only place other than in the church.

Unless they are Sunday school teachers or students, lay people don't talk about their faith all that much at church, either. At worship, they repeat ritual responses and creeds, praying memorized or printed prayers. Their role is primarily one of listening and responding. When it is time for conversation at coffee hour or in the parking lot, the topics are usually practical "how's it going?" or "can you help with ..." exchanges. Members *hear* more church words than they have occasion to *speak* church words.

Church-goers have little practice in applying their knowledge of God (theology) to their everyday life (experience), or to verbalize their thoughts in religious language. The person with the most practice in talking about the Gospel is the pastor. The pastor preaches, prays and teaches. Therefore, members expect their pastors to be full of confident words that can best evangelize newcomers or turn strangers into believers.

Shaking out the third assumption ...

Congregations should draw new people into membership. I began with this assumption, then looked at some ways churches welcome and share the Gospel with outsiders. These are good, well-intended efforts worth continuing. They make a difference in lives of people who might not otherwise know of God's love.

Even so, the reasoning behind the assumption deserves further examination. *If unchurched people would just come into the church building, they would hear the Gospel, enjoy the fellowship and join the church.* The church seems to be the place where the Gospel is on display. The task is to bring people to it. But the Gospel is portable; it was not meant to be contained, but to be carried. I recall the message I saw one day on a sign outside a country church. *The church is intended to be a channel of God's love, not a reservoir.* Congregations are to be Gospel-carriers as well as Gospel-preservers.

Gospel-carriers scattered in the world ...

It is easy to picture the Gospel being proclaimed in the gathered community. Familiar pictures come to mind: the pastor in the pulpit, teachers reading Bible stories to classes of kindergartners, adults meeting for Bible study. This is how the Gospel is proclaimed in the midst of church members.

For a few moments, imagine how the Gospel is proclaimed when members are not together. There is one baptized member out selling real estate to a young couple. Over there are two baptized members running a lawn treatment program with a dozen employees. On another street is a baptized personnel manager in a large retail store. Down the road is a baptized member supervising her children's play with the neighbor's. There are baptized members in hospital beds and nurse's uniforms, teaching school and taking produce to market. This is the scattered church. Everywhere baptized Christians are, there is God's family. They are scattered in the world, disciples carrying the Gospel wherever they go.

The Gospel prompts Christians to live their lives with integrity, do their daily work competently, and treat those around them fairly. They serve God when they provide loving care for those around them. They carry the Gospel into the world by the way they live.

Baptized Christians find ways and times to announce the Gospel, in the midst of their daily lives, too, by both word and deed. The owners of the lawn treatment service make it a practice to employ people who have been down on their luck – helping them re-establish themselves in the community. The personnel manager writes to the corporate vice-president when poorly designed standard forms exclude people he knows would make good employees. The mother, realtor, nurses and others also provide ministry in their work. I know students who went to pray after school with a classmate's mother who has cancer, and a farmer who drops off a portion of his produce at a homeless shelter on his way to the market.

The church has the potential to share the Gospel with all those who have contact with its baptized members. In this electronic age, that even includes one Christian sitting alone at a computer keyboard. Wherever the baptized are, whatever lives they are touching, there is the church. In the article mentioned earlier, J. Paul Rajashekar describes the stretch of the church:

> *The church as a community of believers gathers around the word and sacraments. From this activity, the individual members receive their identity, comfort and nourishment, but all that activity is oriented to a recognition of the latent activity of Christ in the world. If this is not properly understood, Christ's promised identification with the word and sacraments can become distorted into a "church-centered" ecclesiology which is preoccupied primarily with concerns of institutional maintenance, growth, and survival....We need to bear in mind that the church does not control or command the presence of Christ. Rather, the presence of Christ calls forth the church. It is a presence that goes beyond the institutionalized channels and is present even when it is not so named!* [8]

God at work in the world everyday ...

God is busy creating, redeeming and sustaining seven days a week, in both the daylight and night hours. Christians depend on that, whether they give it conscious thought or not. Because God is loving the world every day, the church needs to be pointing that out and celebrating it every day, also. A one-day-a-week churchgoing strategy isn't enough.

God is busy every day, also working in places outside churches – which aren't always so busy from morning to night. God is at work in the places Christians frequent the six other days of the week. If congregations really want to share the Gospel with those who have not heard, they have to do it in places other than the church building. Members need to be Gospel-carrying outsiders.

God's love is loose in the world everyday — sometimes with, and sometimes in spite of, the church's help. Much of God's work happens without church-goers really noticing, and they could become more astute observers of God's actions. With some reflection and practice, they could be quicker to recognize the Gospel when they see it. What would happen if more Christians were to learn to say to their families, neighbors and co-workers, "Look, do you see what God is doing here just now?"

The 3rd Assumption, re-viewed: Congregations should take the "church" to where people are.

A woman in our town did that in a letter to the editor of our local paper. She wrote, saying that when she goes through "a bad patch" in her life, she visits her husband's grave. She was there recently, sobbing, when she heard a woman's voice ask her if she was all right. The letter describes the brief, compassionate exchange between the two women as the true measure and practice of Christianity. The widow noticed what God was doing even in a quiet cemetery, then pointed it out for all of us with newspapers to read.

I began with this old assumption: Congregations should draw new people into membership. *If unchurched people would just come into the church building, they would hear the Gospel, enjoy the fellowship and join the church.* Seeing the assumption from another angle, I might restate it this way: Congregations should take the "church" to where people live their lives.

In other words, *those outside the church need to hear and see the Gospel in everyday places, expressed in everyday words. At some point they may become seekers ready to find a church in which they can learn more.* This is how Gospel-carrying Christians make a difference in the world.

IV. More resources, staff and program

One more assumption spins from the basic one about building strong, growing congregations: Congregations need to increase their resources, staff and program. This reasoning is based on studies of big congregations that continue to attract new members. It says that to *become larger and stronger, churches need to expand worship, education and program opportunities, and that requires more human, financial and physical resources.*

When staff schedules fill up, the nursery room becomes crowded and there is no place to park, growth tapers off. Research documents this trend, and the assumption is that it's time to expand. While most congregations don't envision becoming mega-churches, many see potential for attracting more people into their buildings throughout the week, for which they expect staff to be on hand to lead programs and provide services.

Scope of the program ...

When I began working in congregations, there were committees for Christian education, evangelism, stewardship, social ministry and fellowship. The focus was on members and the content was on commonly accepted congregational functions. A decade later, when I began work in a denominational office, the scope of the congregation's programs had broadened to include issues members faced — such as the death of a spouse, divorce or unemployment. This was the beginning of parenting courses, and by the next decade nursery schools were giving moms a day out, thus supporting working mothers. Soon, friends of members were coming to the support groups and enrolling their children in day care. The programs offered to members and nonmembers continued to expand. Though not uniform across denominations, congregational programming today tends to be custom-made to context. Congregations are much more likely to develop their own resources, or draw from a number of sources, than they were a few decades ago. They value innovative programs or ideas they can adapt to meet their needs.

The 4th Assumption:
Congregations need to increase their resources, staff and program.

The worship life of congregations has also become innovative. "Contemporary" worship is provided along with traditional worship. Sunday morning services are supplemented with worship at other times of day, and other days of the week. Worship planners give more attention to attracting people who cannot come to worship Sunday morning and to those who want to use everyday language and music when they worship.

Professionals and volunteers ...

As congregations add options to worship and programs, the question "Who?" arises. Is this new idea one that the pastor will carry out? What if the pastor doesn't have the time or needed skills?

One traditional answer has been to find a member with the requisite skills and time who will lead the program voluntarily. Mothers who once were music teachers lead children's choirs. Athletically inclined fathers coach softball teams. But who is qualified to lead the support group for grandparents raising young children? Who is willing to supervise a new computer lab program for elementary age children?

My childhood congregation would have had difficulty supplying volunteers for the variety of programs congregations offer now. The number of activities has increased at the same time the pool of volunteers has decreased. Congregations can no longer rely on members to provide all the volunteer services the church needs. There are two reasons, the first of which is time. Most adult members have jobs that demand much of their time. Retirees, who may have more time, often occupy a good portion of it with travel and other interests. The second reason is skill. Volunteers may not have special training required to lead some of the special programs congregations are offering now. Not everyone can be a parish nurse, for instance.

Therefore, the new answer to providing program leadership is to find skilled leaders, pay them for their work, and support them with member volunteers. These skilled people may or may not be clergy. They may or may not be members of the congregation, and the work they undertake may be full-or part-time.

Lay members work with paid staff — serving on committees that oversee programs, giving volunteer time to particular activities, and contributing money for budget support. Some members spend a lot of time and involvement with a variety of church activities. Growing congregations still rely on members to carry out many functions; but the nature and expectations of their involvement are often different and changing. Instead of running programs, members may work with staff to plan, or chair boards that supervise programs.

Remodel, expand or move ...

In addition to finding leaders to staff expanding programs, congregations look for space in which to conduct them. Since most of the activities are on church property, it is natural to assess how ready that is for growth. Can existing space be converted to new uses? Is there room for expansion here, or will it be necessary to relocate?

Congregations seeking to grow try to double up on space. But when the growing weekday nursery school uses all the classroom space, how usable will it be for member children on Sunday? When small groups multiply, are there enough rooms for meetings? When rooms are used two or three times a day, who cleans up after one meeting and sets up for the next?

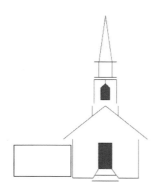

As soon as innovative programming begins, so does the pressure to rethink the use of existing church facilities. Some space can be adapted to multi-purpose use, but other programs require dedicated space — because of the time the program is allotted, the activity involved, or the equipment required. An increase in staff numbers means a need for additional office space and equipment, as well as more demand for custodial services to maintain and keep facilities looking orderly and attractive.

Raising money ...

The capacity of congregations to grow is tied directly to their ability to raise money from their members. The more members in a congregation, the more households there are to sign financial pledge cards. Growing congregations make more growth easier. That fact is depressingly clear to small congregations who have difficulty maintaining property and paying pastors' salaries.

Congregations who have trouble ending the fiscal year in the black are usually those who have trouble imagining themselves growing. By the same token, congregations who have some vision of themselves that stretches beyond their present condition are more likely to raise funds to support that vision. The easiest dollars to raise, of course, are ones for bricks and mortar. People like to see how their money has been spent. They also like to contribute to things they can use. Besides buildings, the benefits of additional staff services and programs can be presented quite clearly.

North Americans give precious little of their wealth to their churches. Poor people are often more generous than rich ones. Nevertheless, there are financial resources available for congregations intent on gathering them. Money usually follows identified needs, not the other way around. Many congregations could improve their financial statements by their membership developing a central vision that makes mission needs clear. It is a rare (and sad?) congregation that has more money than it knows what to do with. Congregations that want to stretch their limits are ones who say so, and then take some risks. Unfortunately, some congregations who have the capacity to grow are too cautious, see only their limitations, and choose to conserve rather than spend.

Shaking out the fourth assumption ...

Congregations need to increase their program, staff and resources. I reasoned earlier that *to become larger and stronger, churches need to expand worship, education and program opportunities, and that requires more human, financial and physical resources.* Compare the congregations in your community that are prospering and those that are declining. There are many examples to support this reasoning.

While "more" feels better, it is no guarantee of either growth or strength. What if I shift the emphasis from becoming larger to becoming stronger? Do churches need the same increases in program, staff and resources? What really prevents congregations from becoming stronger?

Limits to opportunities ...

Some congregations experience property limitations: no room for a parking lot and no way to expand the education building. If the financial picture is good, some may consider relocation, though that will not be an easy discussion. Longtime members have memories tied to the current site, and ministries to the community could be diminished by a move. More often, congregations that feel limited by their facilities turn to modest remodeling as a first step in expanding church programs. That may help — at least temporarily.

However, many congregations feel limited by finances. Those who are not growing usually don't have the assets to compete with larger congregations. Struggling churches know that newcomers usually find larger congregations more attractive. They have more to offer, with more leadership in place and more financial resources to use. Even the smallest congregations feel the pressure to offer more with their limited resources, when at the same time they are being pulled in a conservative, maintenance direction.

Congregations are limited by their vision, too. If they see their task as preserving the past, having resources to maintain property and provide good pastoral services may be all they require. But if their vision includes new opportunities to serve the community, or pushes the boundaries of ministry into daily places, they begin to look for additional resources. Expanding vision removes blinders, and is not put off by limitations.

Putting numbers in their proper place ...

Every congregation has potential to become stronger and grow in spirit. Not all have the same potential to grow in numbers. Shifting the focus from growth to mission in the world can change the way congregations think about resources. It puts numbers in their proper place — as one factor, but not the determining one. There are other resources for doing mission.

Shifting the focus to mission puts all of us church-goers in our proper place—and it is the place of *servant*. When the focus is on growth, we can take a measure of pride when the congregation's statistics show a membership increase. We believe that our skills and leadership help accomplish that goal. But when we consider the trust Christ places in us to represent God in the world, can we have any feelings but humility, awe and dependence on the Holy Spirit? This mission is not something we can do on our own; we serve at God's call and with the Spirit's guidance.

Focus on God's mission puts *all* congregations in their proper place; not just strong, growing ones. Size and potential don't matter; no congregation is exempt from this mission. Small congregations are a means to God's end just as surely as large ones. They don't acquire that responsibility only after reaching a certain size. Opportunities to carry God's love into the world may change as congregations grow, but every congregation does have opportunities.

No congregation of any size or future potential is exempt from this mission.

Congregations growing in membership, and having additional resources to support new buildings and more staff, can be a great resource to their communities and to less well financed churches. While good stewardship of their assets is important, so is the wise use of assets by smaller congregations. Congregations of all sizes, no matter their resources, can deliver God's love in the world. Perhaps larger congregations can work with social service agencies to help dozens of homeless people through bad times. But even very small congregations can provide the family living next door with enough food to get them through the week. Larger congregations may invite neighborhood youth to shoot baskets in their gyms; small congregations can supervise relay races at a local playground at the same time.

One person, from any sized congregation, may be the only one needed to observe juvenile court sessions for a month in order to spotlight the way youth are treated in the justice system. A social activist could ask members to help distribute accurate, balanced information about pending civil-rights legislation. Third-graders can send "welcome" cards to new students in their public school classes. Congregations of any size can provide a breakfast one Sunday in August, inviting their business owners or health care workers (and guests) to talk about how they model Christian behavior in their work and express dilemmas they face.

Focusing on strength for mission redefines the concept of *success* for pastors and congregations. It puts numbers and actions in context. Statistics still count. They remain vital signs, but they are used as they should be – to help understand context and be about mission. Putting numbers in their proper place allows congregations to imagine themselves beyond their current conditions. They are freed to be visionary and encouraged to take risks.

Strengths to strength …

What does it mean to be a strong congregation – even if not one growing in membership?   What would prompt members to say that they
belong to a strong congregation?   Tangible factors are the easiest to name:

- All members worship regularly.
- People of all ages participate in education programs.
- More members contribute an increasingly larger portion of their
  income.

But once again, these are factors that rely on statistical measurements!
What else might members want?   Intangible factors take more thought to
identify, but add important perspective.   Imagine these possibilities:

- a safe place to share both faith and doubts,
- time for reflection and refreshment – a chance to "recharge the bat-
  teries,"
- fellowship with other believers, and support during difficult times,
- opportunities to express and act on Christian values, and
- help in leading a Christian life.

If I were making a list, I know some intangible strengths that I'd be
looking for:

- congregations with a central memory and a vision of mission,
- churches full of Bible students, able to connect scripture with issues
  they face,
- members persistent in prayer and able to pray in public,
- people generous with their gifts, both inside and outside the church,
  and individuals able to see needs and initiate help for the needy.

Think awhile: What else marks a strong congregation?   Make your
own lists.   Look them over and ask, "Do those strengths depend on *more*
programs, or on *carefully-selected* ones?   Do they require *more* staff or *well-
equipped* staff?   Do they call for *more* or *better-used* resources?"

Developing strength may depend more on changing one's view, making bold choices and re-defining expectations.   When congregations
broaden perspective and shake out assumptions they can become more
selective in using their resources.   They may be able to re-negotiate staff
responsibilities and membership roles.   Congregations can become
stronger even without growth when they are clear on God's mission for
the church in their time and place.

While you're making lists, you might make one that notes your congregation's existing strengths; every congregation has some. They are obvious in the gifts of both pastors and lay members, and in existing physical assets and church property. Some strengths are less obvious. Perhaps the building's location lends itself to certain ministries, or there is one program or service that is done well and could be expanded. Consider community and ecumenical contacts that might provide a source of strength by developing partnerships. Look for clusters of members in similar occupations, such as education, health care or law enforcement. Their work may open doors to ministry opportunities.

Untapped resources in members ...

There is another strength every congregation has, but is often slow to recognize. Even congregations who are not growing in membership have a great, underused resource available to them. Gifted members who frequent many daily places are the church's greatest asset. Limits can turn into opportunities when congregations see that they are not restricted by church property lines, building facilities, budgets, income or staff.

Every congregation — whatever its size — is full of human resources. Some churches have little money, poor facilities and part-time pastors. If they can look at themselves from another angle, they will see that they still are rich in resources. They have members with varieties of gifts who are in daily contact with many outsiders. Ask council and committee members how many people they have direct contact with each week — 10? 20? 40? Add up the numbers. They may well exceed your Sunday worship attendance. These members proclaim the Gospel – however haltingly – to more people than the pastor preaches to each week.

Take this example further. Calculate the contacts for the rest of the membership, considering their indirect contacts, too. Gauge such things as services provided by students and members in the community, or the number of people fed by food prepared from crops members produced. Every congregation has a delivery system of Gospel-carriers in place. Even the smallest congregations can exert great influence if they have the courage to do so.

There is no congregation that does not have the resources it needs to carry God's love into its everyday world. Those resources may not be well-polished or may suffer from lack of use, but they exist. Congregations that acknowledge the gifts of baptized ministers in their daily places, and equip members for their daily ministries, can become stronger congregations.

When we understand the mission of the church, and see all those baptized members scattered in the world, new possibilities erase old limitations. The church as institution may not have the influence it once had, but the potential of the scattered church is tremendous. One need not diminish the value of the gathered community to recognize the power of the scattered church when its members are prepared and supported in their everyday ministries.

The 4th Assumption, re-viewed: Congregations need to equip members to minister in God's world.

Don't take the power of the scattered church lightly. I am reminded that the church in mainland China grew in strength and (secretly) in numbers *after* the missionaries had been deported and the church buildings had been confiscated in the Communist takeover. No one knew this until government policy changed, the buildings were returned, and public worship was permitted. Christians are the church even when they cannot go to church.

I began with this assumption: Congregations need to increase their resources, staff and program. *To become larger and stronger, churches need to expand worship, education and program opportunities and that requires more human, financial and physical resources.* Having seen the old assumption from another angle I might restate it this way: Congregations need to equip members to minister in God's world.

North American culture values bigness in homes, cars, dinner plate portions and business deals. Bigness is not wrong, but it is not the only way to success. Churches do not need to grow in size to be effective centers for mission. Nor is growth a guarantee that churches will be effective. *Congregations become stronger when they recognize that members are their greatest resource for doing mission, and when they concentrate on encouraging, equipping and supporting members in their everyday ministries.*

A Summary of Inside/Outside Assumptions

Well-worn assumptions	...re-viewed
I. Congregations should grow in numbers and strength. *The greater the number of church members, the wider the knowledge of the Gospel in the community.*	I. Congregations should carry God's love into the World. *Congregations are "commissioning centers" – one of the means God uses to deliver the Gospel in particular places, in partnership with other groups, and through daily discipleship of members.*
II. Members should go to church regularly. *People who really believe the Gospel will express their faith by worshiping weekly and participating in other church activities.*	II. Members should be the Church always. *People who are baptized will express their faith when they gather with other Christians inside the church, and when they use their gifts to serve God in their daily places.*
III. Congregations should draw new persons into membership. *If unchurched people would just come into the church building, they would hear the Gospel, enjoy the fellowship and join the church.*	III. Congregations should take the "church" to where people are. *Those outside the church need to see the Gospel in everyday places, and hear it shared with everyday words. At some point they may become seekers ready to find a church in which they can learn more.*
IV. Congregations need to increase their resources, staff and program. *To become larger and stronger, churches need to expand worship, education and program opportunities that require more human, financial and physical resources.*	IV. Congregations need to equip members to minister in God's world. *Congregations become stronger when they recognize that members are their greatest resource for doing mission, and concentrate on encouraging, equipping and supporting members in their everyday ministries.*

End notes

4   David Coffin, Montpelier, Ohio in a letter published in *Lutheran Partners*, July-August 2000.

5   J. Paul Rajashekar, *Church as a Community of Ex-centric People, Parish Practice Notebook*, p.1. Andrew White, ed. Spring, 1996. LTSP.

6. Lutheran Book of Worship, p.124.

7   The Rev. Alice Platt. Unpublished letter. 1997.

8. J. Paul Rajashekar, *Parish Practice Notebook*, p.2, 3. Andrew White, ed. Spring, 1996. LTSP.

Chapter 5

Identify the ministers

The question I keep asking is "How could we do things differently inside to better carry God's love outside?" One answer that keeps coming back is: *by taking the ministry of both clergy and laity seriously.* I believe my answer is the key to making congregations a powerful force for change, and a realistic way to carry healing and peace into God's world. The first step is to comprehend that members really are ministers.

The Sunday Gary preached

The church of which I am a member is one of two linked small congregations — a town church and a country church served by one full-time pastor. During the "pastoral vacancy" created by the pastor's resignation last spring, a retired clergy person provided interim pastoral services. He and other retired pastors conducted most of the worship, but occasionally lay members, such as Martha and her husband, Gary, led worship.

On one Sunday last summer, Gary stood in front of the congregation to make announcements. Introducing himself, he said humorously — and for the benefit of visitors — "Don't worry, I'm not the minister here." People chuckled. We all understood what he meant.

Martha led us through the liturgy and read the lessons. Then Gary stood before the congregation again — this time to preach. The day's lessons led easily to a focus on hearing God's call. Gary examined those scripture passages. He told about two specific times in his life when he had heard God's call. He listed many ways members respond to God's call as they serve the church – teaching, singing in the choir, ushering. He raised good questions. He made me think. It was a fine sermon.

Clearly, Gary's faith in God is real. He has experienced God's intervention in what was a dangerous moment in his life. Gary thinks about God in relationship to his future as well as his past. He believes that God will provide for him and will "call him home" to be with God forever. Meanwhile, Gary does most of the church things he listed in the sermon. He and Martha are very active in the life of our congregation, and take seriously their commitment to serve.

Gary isn't a minister in our church? Of course he is! Along with Martha and many other people. We just happen to be a group of ministers temporarily without a pastor. Both clergy and laity have ministering roles to play in carrying out the church's mission.

Laity and clergy – insiders and outsiders

Shaking out assumptions about "church" and "mission" leads to taking a second look at the people classified as clergy and laity. That means a couple of old stereotypes need to be addressed. One is that the pastor is the *only* minister. The other is that *everything* that pastors do is ministry.

The ministry of the laity – nice, but peripheral ...

The church talks a lot about pastors being called to the ministry. They are typically designated "ministers" by title. Where does that leave the laity? As those ministered unto? Or, as I heard one pastor describe them in a sermon, as "part-time" ministers? The notion that lay people minister is sometimes treated as an after-thought or add-on, not something to take seriously.

When the subject of the laity's ministry comes up in gatherings of church types, what frequently occurs is benevolent "glazing-over." For many, the topic does not seem on a par with serious issues facing the church. Listeners will smile, nod their heads and agree. After all, how do you argue with the idea that God *does* something at baptism, that God *expects* something from those baptized?

What these insiders fail to see is that the *reason* for one of the most serious issues facing the church is also one of its *best solutions*. Church leaders worry about membership decline. They talk about how hard it is to find enough qualified members to teach Sunday school, serve on committees and keep the choir going. They are concerned about the people who tell Gallup pollsters that they are Christians, but in fact rarely attend church. There is good reason to worry.

These church leaders have looked at the church so long
from the insider's position that they find it difficult to see
why lay members are not more faithful and responsive.
If those leaders would look at the church from the lay
members' place on the outside edge, they might see
things differently.

People who experience church more as a place
where they are to give time and money, rather than a
community in which they receive nourishment, are not likely to come to
church as often. People seek communities in which they are valued, and
from which they receive energy, satisfaction and support — places where
they are needed and respected, but not used. Too often, lay people find
congregations are more interested in what they can do for the church than
in what the church can offer them. When the pastor or council president
calls, it's more likely he or she is recruiting members to do a church task,
rather than checking on how things are going with the new boss at work.

The ministry of the laity – outside …

The church sometimes acknowledges the ministries of lay members
inside the congregation, but has virtually ignored their ministries outside
the congregation. A succession of pastors, Sunday school teachers, parents and other church members have indoctrinated people like Gary to
reserve the term "minister" for pastors. They have taught people like
Gary that good church members are active inside — with choir, committees, Sunday school and regular worship attendance.

Betty was an instructor in the community nursing school. When I
worked in her congregation years ago, I was focused on the inside ministries of that church. Because of her work with nursing students, I
thought she would be great as an advisor for our senior high youth program. I asked; she turned me down flat.

Several months later, I visited Betty in the community hospital. She
had just had a mastectomy. While I was there, several nursing students
stopped to see her. When they left, she told me that she had been talking
to these students about her surgery, helping them understand what she –
the patient – was going through. Then, she explained that those women
were the reason she had said "no" to me. She spent extra time with them,
and gave them all she had so that they might be the best nurses possible.

Betty exercised her baptismal call in order that others would tend the sick competently and compassionately.

Our congregation did not recognize her ministry. She was considered "semi-active", an occasional worshiper. They understood that the pastor, when preaching the Word on Sunday morning, was God's representative. They didn't realize that Betty was also God's representative while she worked with nursing students. No one ever told members that they were God's people while they were dealing with personnel problems at work on Monday, or sitting on the local zoning board on Tuesday night. Someone should have.

There is no Christian without a call to minister. God issues the call in baptism. It applies to all aspects of living, including occupations. Some Christians choose to represent God as ordained ministers. Other Christians represent God while working as zoo keepers, hotel maids, hairdressers, financial advisors, professional athletes or grain elevator operators. The call is the same; the arenas and tasks are different. It is high time church leaders get that message out; then, behave as if they believe it was important.

Demonstrate through words and actions ...

Talking about the ministry of the baptized is not enough. It must be reinforced by attitudes and behavior; otherwise it is just lip service. Pastors who habitually ask members about the issues in their workplaces demonstrate — by their interest — that those places are really important. When they weave those issues into sermons, members know they have been heard. Churches who form Sunday prayers around weekday concerns show members that what they do Monday through Saturday is valuable. When the petitions are specific, they sound real. It's fine to pray for farming in general, but it hits home in my community when we pray about drought, toxic runoffs or fungi attacking the corn crop.

Ed, a pastor of a large suburban congregation, admitted to me that he once considered himself an advocate for the ministry of the baptized because he preached about it occasionally and encouraged members to come in work clothes on Labor Day Sunday. He never understood why the idea hadn't sparked much member interest.

His "Aha!" moment arrived while he was trying to recruit the principal of a middle school to chair the Christian education committee. He had his list of reasons ready. He knew it would be a tough sell because there were some big problems brewing at the school. He began by asking the principal how things were going. That was his undoing as a salesman, but it opened his eyes as a pastor. He found himself listening to someone stressed and short of time, doing work that made a difference to church families and to the community. Why was the church – why was *he* – adding pressure right now, instead of relieving it?

It suddenly dawned on the pastor that he was always recruiting people to do church jobs — from ushering to teaching to planning the Christmas program – with little regard to their other life demands. He might be preaching that ministry in the world was important, but by his actions he had been teaching people that what was really important was keeping the church going.

Respecting weekday pressures does not mean pastors should hold back from asking busy laity to do church things. While people need to decide their own response, pastors can make it easier to say "no" without feeling guilty. Congregational leaders can relieve the pressure on members to give more time at church by recognizing the importance of their ministries on the *outside*, as well as on the *inside*. They can encourage people to use their gifts in community causes rather than adding another social ministry program at church. The pastor can meet the evangelism committee chair at her place of work to plan the next meeting agenda, rather than asking her to stop at church on her way home. The council can revise meeting schedules so families make fewer trips to the church building.

Congregations can recognize both the call to ministry of all the baptized, and the specific arenas in which they minister. The church can support the daily ministry of the laity, even as the laity supports the ministries of the church. Both are important.

The daily places of pastors – on the outside …

While, errantly, laity sometimes may be seen as part-time ministers, clergy could be described as over-timers in the eyes of many lay people who believe that pastors work for the church 24 hours a day. Some clergy foster the notion that pastors are always on call, with calendars that are crammed with meetings and appointments throughout the week.

This long-held image of the overtime pastor is re-enforced by the fact that most lay people see their pastor only at church. That place, and the work that goes on there, seems to consume the pastor's whole life. For members who are workaholics, it is fairly easy to project their own job absorption into their pastor's devoted attention to church work.

Recently, seminary courses and continuing education seminars have been teaching pastors about self-care and setting boundaries. To be good stewards of their own lives, pastors need time for family, friends, exercise and recreation. To find that time, they need to set limits on the days and hours they are available to parishioners each week. While emergencies will interrupt their personal schedules at times, setting a pattern of both work and personal time is important to having healthy, effective pastors.

One of the ways congregations minister to their pastors is to encourage them to take care of themselves. An active personnel or pastoral support committee can provide ongoing attention to the well-being of all professional staff that the congregation employs. It can advise the pastor and other staff on priority use of their time. If pastors are to have time to themselves, they probably have to take that time from congregational activities. Congregations minister by making those choices with their pastors.

The church has acknowledged the need for self-care and boundary-setting for its pastors. It has not yet recognized that pastors are really lay people in some aspects of their daily lives. The spotlight has been on what pastors do inside their congregations. Their roles as spouses, parents, citizens, consumers, neighbors and volunteers remain in the shadows. The church could minister to pastors by validating the outside dimensions of pastors' lives.

Pastors and laity frequent some of the same daily places. They are both consumers at the grocery store and shopping mall. In the community, both are citizens and neighbors. At the park or swimming pool, both seek refreshment and recreation. The outside dimensions of clergy lives are as legitimate as their pastoral roles. They should not have to apologize for taking time away from the church. Pastors should not feel guilty about going to PTA meetings or rehearsing with a barbershop quartet. It's time for lay members to stop raising their eyebrows or gossiping about their pastors' outside activities. Instead, they should be inviting their pastors to attend concerts with them, and cheering them on when they run five miles in charity races.

Members and pastors can find common ground in their mutual interests as lay persons. Both care about high quality schools for their children and look for good doctors, plumbers and dry cleaners. Both have opinions about government plans and legislation that affect their community. The everyday life of pastors bridges easily with that of their parishioners. They have much in common that they discuss very little. When laity and clergy get together they talk about church. Maybe it's time to change that.

I began this section with two stereotypes. One is that the pastor is the only minister — a poor characterization because it ignores the fact that laity minister daily. The second is that pastors are always ministering. While closer to the truth, it needs clarification. Pastors minister professionally as church leaders working on the inside. They also minister personally as lay persons in their private, outside lives.

The roles of laity and clergy

The way members see the church often dictates expectations of how clergy and laity are to behave when they are at the church. I described some traditional views of their roles in Chapter 2. When congregations begin to shake out assumptions, however, they also begin to shake up their understandings of the ministry roles of clergy and laity. The following chart outlines some differences that may emerge.

Pastors and lay people are partners in a mission enterprise. Both have important, though complementary roles, neither of which is in competition with the other. In fact, if they are to carry out their roles well, each needs the other.

Pastors still are responsible for leading worship, preaching and administering the sacraments. They are responsible for teaching, studying, visiting, counseling, marrying, burying, organizing and administering. Lay members still have roles as musicians, lectors, ushers, teachers, students, planners, implementers and decision-makers. Two other roles become visible for the laity, also.

The Roles of Clergy and Laity Inside and Out

Well-worn assumptions	... from a new angle
I. Pastors are in charge of the mission. *They are the most knowledgeable and best qualified to set the direction and to call on members to help.*	I. Laity are equally responsible for the mission. *They are knowledgeable about mission in the world and have the most access to those outside the church.*
II. Pastors are the ministers. *Their ordination gives them the authority to minister.*	II. All Christians are ministers. *Their baptism gives both clergy and laity the authority to minister.*
III. Pastors carry out the congregation's mission with laity support. *They are official leaders of congregations and bear primary responsibility for what is accomplished.*	III. Lay people carry out the mission with the support of clergy. *They have the most opportunity to deliver God's love in the world, while their pastors teach, encourage and support them.*
IV. Lay members use their gifts primarily in the church's programs. *Their gifts are best used in the congregation's ongoing program, which is the main way laity support the mission of the church.*	IV. Lay members uses their gifts most often in their daily places. *Their gifts are most often used in their daily places of family, community and work, which are their main arenas for doing mission.*
V. Pastors are the evangelists who attract outsiders into the church. *Clergy are the main reason new people come to church. Their preaching and personal attention turn visitors into members.*	V. Lay members are the evangelists in whom outsiders see God's love. *Laity represent the church as they express their faith in words and caring deeds during their daily contacts with the unchurched.*
VI Pastors are full-time ministers. *Their work for the church goes on 24-hours a day, seven days a week. Lay persons, on the other hand, minister part-time through church programs and charitable activities.*	VI. All Christians minister full-time. *Both pastors and lay members minister inside the church. Both minister on the outside, too. Pastors are lay persons in their families and communities.*

Informed lay interpreters inside …

Lay people assume the role of interpreters of the outside world within the gathered community. They have the "view from the edge" that I described earlier. They stand on the inside rim of the church. They see the world as believers who are well aware of what it means to make one's way on the outside, daily.

When lay people share their knowledge of daily life as they see outsiders living it, they help the congregation shape its mission in the world. They keep the church on course. Being part of the gathered community allows laity to step aside from their daily places, but it does not mean they should forget those daily places.

Members have valuable information about the world. They have contacts there in the church's mission field. Members are in touch with the new imperatives in their communities. They see, firsthand, the socio-economic changes that affect their neighborhoods, towns or counties. Pastors discover some of this piece-meal, through their own daily lives or when they see FOR SALE signs or hear members have lost jobs. But how often do congregations marshal the information members have about neighborhoods, work sites, local government issues and social service priorities? I'm stressing perspective again, because congregations are full of people whose world-wisdom is rarely tapped. It's time to change that.

If members could share their knowledge, and congregations had practice in making the most of differences, they might learn some valuable things. For example, their shared knowledge would tell planners whether they need to prepare for growth or decline in the church's finances.

Members should be on the lookout for human needs and mission opportunities when they are outside the church. What they discover outside should be a major topic of discussion, reflection and prayer when they come back inside. If the church is to be Gospel-carrying, the daily worlds of members afford many opportunities for delivering God's love.

Sharing what's happening in their everyday worlds, lay people provide clues to what they need in their church worlds, too. Their experience should find its way into Sunday sermons, congregational prayers, education programs and support systems. How can congregations turn church-going members into Gospel-carrying outsiders if they don't know what is going on in their members' daily places?

Informed Gospel-carriers outside …

Lay people assume another role, that of insiders who interpret the church to outsiders. They are evangelists and Gospel-carriers. That's different from being members of an evangelism committee that is preparing plans to attract new people into church to hear the Gospel. The laity is the church's delivery system for taking God's love into the world. It's not really a new role, but it will be news to many lay people. The idea of ministering on their own will surprise many of them. It's not that they aren't doing it already. They are. It's just that many of them have not heard it named "ministry" before. Over and over, I've seen amazement and excitement in the eyes of lay people when they realize that they are baptized ministers.

The notion that all Christians minister may not be good news to everyone in the congregation. It is easier for some to put all the responsibility for ministering on the pastor's shoulders. Their attitude is that this is what pastors are paid to do. They would rather not have to re-examine God's expectations of them. It's less demanding for the church to serve them when they want it, than to be God's servants wherever they go. People who have been raised with this "consumer" view of the church will need time and re-assurances before they will accept a different view.

But many church members will be invigorated when they discover they are partners in the church's mission. They have always understood that they are part of the gathered church, but they are used to doing ministry through the congregation's organized programs. While they will need frequent reminders in order to become accustomed to the idea that they minister outside of church, they will see new potential in their daily routines. They will make the connection between going to church and being a baptized Christian with a mission. Daily life gives them repeated opportunities.

Pete is a curator. He sees the connection. In an Advent devotional booklet last year, he wrote, "Sometimes it can be hard, at first glance, to see how you can be carrying out the Lord's calling in an ordinary job. I, for instance, work for a museum. When I do my job well, nobody gets fed, or gets a roof over his head, or gets over an illness. I am charged with caring for objects, not people. In an already-too-materialistic society, how can that meet God's purposes for me?

"Actually, I do not merely preserve objects, but record memories and stories of people, living and dead, who are associated with those objects. Moreover, I use those memories and stories for education, not only for the school age visitors, but for people who want to continue learning throughout their lives. In the course of my day, I have dozens of opportunities to treat other people in a fair, helpful, forgiving, generous or kind way. That, I find, is important to my work for God in this world."[9]

Members who will be glad to hear that they minister in their daily places will still hesitate about talking about their faith. One woman told me recently that she just doesn't know a lot about the Bible and doesn't want to force it on others. Many active church members worry that they are not educated in scripture and, therefore, are not sure-tongued about sharing the Gospel. Either they don't feel they know the Bible well enough, or they cringe at the thought of "witnessing" in the manner of those strangers who have confronted them on street corners or at their front doors.

Pastors can help dispel this notion. Gospel-carriers need not be Bible experts, just Bible students. They don't need to confront strangers. Their best opportunities come when they can respond to people they know using words and actions with which they are comfortable.

Different teaching roles for clergy ...

Equipping lay people for ministry defines a role for pastors that may be new to some church-goers. It is the role of the teaching coach. Pastors need to teach about the faith in ways that will help lay people develop their own skills as Bible scholars. Pastors need to help people practice telling the Good News and praying in their own words if they are to be Gospel-carriers in the world.

It's not enough for the pastor to be a good scholar who can interpret scripture to members. Members need to learn how to interpret scripture themselves, so they can share their ideas with others. That calls for a teaching style that shows learners how to study and figure things out for themselves. It's not enough for the pastor to be facile at prayer when the occasion calls for it. Members need to learn how to pray spontaneously *in* church if they are to pray confidently with others *outside* church. It's not enough for pastors to have theological responses to life's difficult times and tragedies. Members, especially teens and adults, need opportunities to talk about real everyday situations so they can respond to outsiders who are facing such situations.

The role of the pastor is to be the teacher of evangelists, rather than the congregation's *chief* evangelist. Pastors fulfill that role by being both preacher and coach. That means proclaiming the Gospel in sermons week after week, and equipping laity to identify the Gospel as they experience it day after day. Pastors carry both the responsibility to speak the Word to the gathered community themselves, and the task of equipping the gathered community to speak it to others.

Lay members are the Gospel-carriers who spend most of their time among people who don't know God's love. By the time outsiders venture into church, they have heard something about a loving God that makes them want to know more. They are ready for more formal instruction in the Word. When outsiders become seekers, the pastor becomes a "teaching evangelist" to the seekers. The pastor's preaching — as well as personal visits, conversations and member classes — provides this instruction.

Pastoral role of guidance counselor, too ...

Clergy need to be guidance counselors as well as teaching coaches. They are usually skilled in helping laity recognize how their gifts could be used inside church, but Gospel-carrying outsiders may need help in seeing how their gifts are used for ministry in the world. The pastor who was recruiting the school principal was just discovering his role as a guidance counselor. I recall another pastor who pointed out to one member that her organizing skills could be applied to establishing a hospice program in their small community. I know of a third pastor who makes a practice of encouraging teenage members to do volunteer service at the police association's boy's club. These pastors are guiding members to use their gifts where they can be most beneficial, rather than cultivating the gifts for church use only.

Pastors are guidance counselors, also, when they help individual members connect their daily work with ministry. I'm thinking of a church member who works as a cashier at the superstore on the highway. She hums Gospel tunes as she works, and she has an engaging "gift of gab" that spills out up and down her checkout line. What if her pastor helped her realize that she may be the only person some of those customers will meet that day — or that week — who smiles at them and treats them with kindness? What if she learned that she could give that man who's always so shabbily dressed a voucher for the ecumenical thrift shop? Pastors can affirm the gifts members employ in their outside places and make them more aware of specific opportunities available to them.

If the congregation's mission extends to all the places members are during the week, the pastor needs to become familiar with these places. Some are places pastors frequent in the course of their own daily lives as parents, consumers, citizens and householders. But to learn about other daily places of members, pastors need to become students and invite members to be their teachers.

The goal: Gospel-carriers

When baptized Christians go to church, they seek worship that restores and comforts them in language they understand. They want their faith and courage renewed, so they are ready to face the challenges of their daily lives. They depend on their pastors to make worship significant.

For many baptized Christians, when they leave church their worship is over until next week. Some are so busy during the week that they give little thought to Bible reading and prayer, let alone private meditation or reflection. Many have never learned how to find scripture passages or formulate prayers.

If going to church is enough, there would be little reason to teach people how to pray or search scripture. But if baptized Christians have ministry to do in the world, they will need to pray for themselves, and perhaps with others. There will be situations that send them searching scripture for guidance. Lay members who understand that they are Gospel-carriers will see more reason to become regular students of the Bible or join a prayer group. They will seek worship practices that sustain them in their daily work. They will expect their congregations to be resources for, rather than refuges from, daily life.

I believe that the more aware members are of their ministry roles on the outside, the more they will cherish their time inside the church. Being the scattered church knits them more closely to the gathered church. Though separated from the gathered community physically most of the week, they are tied together by their common calling. When that sense develops in a congregation, gathering times become opportunities to share what happened in the past week's pursuit of ministry. Prayers are offered in celebration and supplication, and learning from each other, people bolster their own courage. The congregation regains some of the characteristics of the 1st Century church.

In congregations that have turned mission inside-out, the church building takes on the added function of a practice field or rehearsal hall. Pastors who accept the roles of teaching coach and guidance counselor create opportunities for members to talk about the changes they see in their daily places, and about other life issues. They set aside time to pray and read scripture together. Such "practice" times nourish disciples, building their confidence and courage as Gospel-carriers. Describing Christians as believers who *practice* their faith takes on a whole new meaning.

Practice steps …

Practicing the faith includes at least four elements. Any of the steps can be initiated by asking simple questions.

1. Recognize ministries already happening.

Church-goers need to become aware of the ways they currently carry the Gospel into the world. "What did you do last Tuesday?" the pastor might ask. "What ministry was happening in your Tuesday's activities?" By practicing with more questions and sharing the stories that emerge, lay people will see that living their lives with integrity, and doing their work competently, is a form of service and sharing the Gospel. It is God-pleasing.

Sandi manages employee insurance for a large school system in San Antonio. Her daily office work was interrupted frequently by phone calls from teachers who had not read memos, filled out forms or didn't know how to file a claim. Making the connection between work and faith made a big difference to her. She realized that the calls for help were not intrusions but opportunities to minister. Now, she sits down to her desk praying that she can be helpful. Her attitude has changed, and people notice the difference. Instead of leaving the office at the end of the day frustrated about interrupted work, she leaves feeling she has been of service.

Alberto is a police officer in the Virgin Islands. When he first heard that all baptized Christians minister he became depressed. It seemed like a burden. He felt as if he had just acquired a second daily job. But his pastor and some friends reminded him of stories he had told them about his daily work. They helped him to see how his fairness and humanity toward those facing criminal charges was motivated by his Christian faith. They told him that the way he dealt with the poorest and least of society had been an inspiration to them.

Suddenly, a smile broke out on Alberto's face. It was one job he had to do each day after all, and he did it as a Christian. "This is deep," he kept repeating. "If this is true, it touches everything about my life."

2. Look for God's work and name it.

Secondly, learn to recognize God's activity in the world and describe it with everyday words. What was God doing in the heavy rains and flooding last week, in a 3rd grade classroom, on planes flying coast-to-coast or at the golf course? Practice observing God at work in the world and reflecting on what this says about the nature of God.

God's daily work is the Gospel; Christians need only point it out. They do not have to be experts in scripture or doctrine to share what they see God doing daily. They don't need advanced degrees or a four-syllable religious word vocabulary to carry the Gospel into the world. They do need practice using ordinary language to talk about their faith. Everyday language that outsiders understand is the best way to talk about faith when opportunities arise.

Alice was a poet. Her writing was simple, but clearly expressive of her faith. She put her poems inside get-well cards. I often saw her at the bus stop with simple bouquets of flowers, waiting for a ride to the hospital. Members of our congregations, friends and acquaintances, even friends-of-friends were blessed by a few moments of Alice's time, her flowers and her words of faith.

3. Realize that outsiders are persons known, not strangers.

Next, Gospel-carrying outsiders need to realize that most of the outsiders with whom they are in contact are not strangers. They are people with whom they have some relationship. Who is in your car pool; how is life going for them? Who have you met in your new aerobics class; what kind of schedules are they trying to juggle? How do other members of the Chamber of Commerce feel about the vandalism that has been on the rise at the mall? Practice identifying people who are part of members' everyday lives, and imagining ways to carry the Gospel to them.

The old images of going from door-to-door in strange neighborhoods or standing on the street corner are poor images of Gospel-carriers. People in those images tend to be Gospel-pushers or membership recruiters. They are not interested in meeting people where they are, but in taking them to where they want them to be.

Gospel-carriers, on the other hand, take God's Word and healing love to people they know in the midst of situations they are facing. They are not hunting for new members to swell the ranks of their congregations. Instead, they are looking for ways to bring God's Word to bear in their daily places. They act out of compassion and on behalf of justice, so they are free to relate to people they know — using everyday language and behaving in ordinary ways. Their conversations need not be intellectual, academic ones, but spontaneous exchanges in which they share their observations and feelings in everyday words. These do not need to be long, complicated conversations. They are not contests to win but gifts to offer.

Jan is a lay person who is comfortable sharing her faith. She told me she'd circulated a petition about a municipal matter in her community. Some of the neighbors she visited shared problems they were facing. Before she left their homes, she told those neighbors that she would be glad to pray for them if they would like for her to do that. Jan told me no one ever said "no", even if they were not church-goers.

Lynette has an important marketing job in a major corporation. She was relieved when she learned that lay people are called to minister in the world. She was never a "big church activity person." Her career demands and other interests meant that she spent most of her time outside the church – feeling guilty that she wasn't in more church activities. Once she grasped the idea of being a Gospel-carrier outside, she began to see possibilities.

A big one presented itself when a good friend of her teenage son landed in jail. She saw it as a challenge from God. During the time the young man was incarcerated, she wrote and visited. When he was released someone asked him what Lynette had done to help him. He replied that she had accepted him for who and where he was. She did not judge or preach at him. She ministered to him as a peer, sharing what was going on in her life as well as listening to his struggles and fears.

4. Learn that both words and actions convey the Gospel.

Finally, members learn that actions may well come before words. How did you treat your classmates on Thursday? What was your reaction to the cranky customer? Why did you take time for your long-winded neighbor? Members practice identifying behavior that conveys God's love. Acts of patience and compassion deliver the Gospel even if words are not spoken. Actions speak louder than words. Acts of ministry command attention, opening the door to conversations when the time is right.

Jack and Sarah run a landscaping and lawn care business. When they heard that the mother of one of their daughter's classmates had terminal cancer, they helped in the way they knew best. Though never having met the family, they looked after the mother's garden and filled the yard in early spring with her favorite pansies.

Jan is a stay-at-home mom. A person strong in her faith, she became friends with Jean, a lapsed member from another denomination, when their children were in the same day-care center. The two women began to help each other with car pooling and baby-sitting. Recently, Jean said to Jan, "Tell me about your God." When Jan and I talked about this later she was joyful about the invitation and very clear on one point. She was not sharing her faith in the hope that Jean would then want to come to Jan's church. Her hope was simply that Jean was ready to re-establish her relationship with God. If she returned to her own church, wanted to come with Jan, or was only ready to talk about God, that was fine.

An American Christian taught English as a second language in China. Legally, not able to talk about her faith, she shared it through lovingly treating her students. She was confident they sensed the Gospel in her. Her hope was that they would long for a community in which they could find similar fellowship and support. That, she believed, would draw them to the church.

My husband and I worshiped in a congregation in Nanjing during a visit to China years ago. As with every worship service we attended during that trip, we were amazed at the numbers present and felt a sense of hospitality and belonging. When we walked into the courtyard after the service, we noticed several tables set up in a long row with chairs on either side. This was called the "Inquirer's Table" by our guides. Chinese Christians could not proclaim the Gospel to their neighbors, but if those neighbors chose to come to church, they could ask about Christianity. So each Sunday, church members sat on one side of that table ready to share their faith. Seekers came to the other side with their questions. The American teacher was correct. The fellowship and support God's love generates among believers is recognized by outsiders. It draws people to it. Those who know the Gospel communicate it to others – almost in spite of themselves.

Lay members have the most opportunities to perform ordinary acts of Christian love with people at times when they are most ready to receive them. Their deeds may be simple acts of kindness, but they are done in the name of Christ. Lay people exemplify the love of Christ to their neighbors. It may take a cup of cold water, a warm coat or, as with Lynette, visits to jail. The role of the laity is taking the Gospel to people who need it right where they are. This is what baptized Christians do now. Their pastors help them do it with more confidence and sense of mission.

Beyond the "sheep" thing ...

The roles of clergy and laity inside the gathered community really do not change much, but the content and context in which they carry out their roles do. Pastors preach in ways that speak directly to members' daily lives because they know their work places and neighborhoods. Pastors suggest reshaping programs to place more focus on outside situations that members have been telling them about.

The central role of the pastor in the congregation's gathered life remains vital. Pastors call members together for praise, thanksgiving, forgiveness, proclamation and renewal. Pastors equip lay people for ministering required outside. Lay members rely on their pastors to help them sort through everyday dilemmas and opportunities, give them encouragement, and call them back to their Lord in worship.

A Minnesota pastor summed it in a group evaluation meeting by noting that pastors need to teach all members to be leaders. She said that churches have to get beyond this "sheep" thing. Clergy teach leadership through their preaching styles and by their ability to be mentors, coaches and facilitators. She wasn't disparaging the recurring Biblical image of shepherd and flock that has become one traditional way to define the pastor's role. She *was* saying that it's not an adequate image. Christians live their lives outside the fold. They are not mindless followers but gifted, baptized children of God.

The example of Jesus sending out his disciples serves as a better image of the roles of laity and clergy for a church turned inside-out. In his ninth chapter, Luke reports that Jesus gave the disciples power and authority, then sent them out to heal and proclaim the kingdom of God. That puts it clearly – unless demons and curing diseases become a stumbling block! The pastor's role is to empower members to use their gifts in order to live out their baptismal calling. The pastor is to equip members with the authority of God's Word. The laity's role is to deliver the Good News to their villages in words and through healing actions.

The story in Luke does not end with the disciples going out; they came back and told Jesus all that they had done. Church is coming back to tell what happened. Church is coming back to learn from and support each other. Church is time to turn over to God successes and failures, to seek forgiveness and renewed faith.

The title of this book sets out an unfair distinction. Congregations need to be groups of church-going insiders *and* Gospel-carrying outsiders. The problem is that some congregations have behaved as if they had a choice. They have put all their efforts into winning church-going insiders, but this is not an either-or proposition. Congregations need to put equal energy into nurturing Gospel-carrying outsiders. It will turn churches inside-out.

End note

9 Pete Lesher. Unpublished Advent Devotional Booklet. 2000. Grace Lutheran Church. Easton, MD.

3rd Idea:
Start with simple changes

Chapter 6

Re-balance the mission

In this book's introduction, I described the church's mission strategy as (too often) "one location, one-day-a-week, Christian-to-Christian." We insiders spend most of our energy and resources on activities that happen within church walls — among members — on Sundays and some week nights. Pastors may preach about serving neighbors, children may color place mats for nursing homes, women may sew quilts for overseas missions, but they do it at church with other Christians. While allusions may be made to serving God outside the church walls, the experiences these church members associate with serving God are church activities. Mission is what happens at church. I don't minimize the value of those inside activities; many good things *do* happen at church. But I want church-goers to see that mission is what happens *after* church, also. And they have to be taught that concept while they are at church.

"How could we do things differently *inside* to better carry God's love *outside*?" One practical answer to that question is: *by giving equal attention, in church programs and mission statements, to carrying the Gospel to everyday, outside places.* Show how mission happens in the world. Link inside experiences directly to real outside places. Shift the balance of inside activities to shed light outside. Any congregation – no matter its size – can do this.

A balancing act

I watched three boys playing in the park one day. One, settling into the seat on the "grounded" side of a see-saw, called for his friends to take the upended seat on the other side. Between them, they pulled it down while the first boy stood over the other seat — his feet on the ground — and helped them bring their side down within their reach. Of course, then both boys wanted to climb on, and when they did, suddenly the first boy was clinging to his seat, which was now high in the air. At the same time, the two boys who shared the same seat hit the ground with a thud. All three laughed and giggled. Such fun! This was exactly what they had expected.

Then one of the boys on the grounded side got off and ran to the other side. His companions balanced the see-saw so he could board. The result was the same — in reverse. More laughter. This went on for five or ten minutes — one boy flying high while the other two hit the dust. There was pushing and squirming as each boy jockeyed for a better position.

Finally, the smallest boy, grounded on the two-seater side, started to pull himself upward on see-saw's balancing arm. Nothing changed at first; one playmate was stuck in the air, the other in the dirt. Then as the small boy shinnied up the beam further, something exciting happened. His partner's feet no longer touched the ground. Their buddy's seat was coming down, and when the small boy neared the center of the see-saw, both sides were even. The boy in one seat could push with his feet to send himself upward and bring the boy in the other seat downward. These were little boys who probably had not heard the word "physics" yet, but they were having a wonderful time exploring the notion of balance.

At some time during their youth, in playgrounds or physics classes, children learn how to balance weights to keep the action going. If all the weight is over the fulcrum there is no leverage to put the see-saw into motion. If too much weight is at one end, action stops. The "up" end is useless until more weight is added to balance the weight at the other end.

When congregations share perspectives and shake out assumptions, they may realize that one dimension of being the church has overshadowed others. They may discover that one approach to serving God's mission has gotten out-of-balance. They can restore action by changing focus or adding new possibilities.

See-saws illustrate the importance of balance. If there is no balance, the see-saw is stuck. Comparable weights on both sides provide the balance needed to generate action. The weights may seem to work against each other but, in fact, the pressure one side exerts against the other gives the second side enough momentum to exert pressure, also.

If congregations could see the world as mission locations — as well as their churches — they would gain new momentum. They would come "unstuck" from longstanding patterns. Ministry that occurs within the gathered community becomes one weight on the see-saw. Ministry by the scattered community in the world becomes the balancing weight. Both are valuable. What takes place inside the church propels members outside for daily ministry, and daily experiences send them back inside to be recharged for another week. The see-saw is moving. Congregations experience renewing energy.

The see-saw is a good image to underline the value of the differing perspectives and momentum balance can generate. It also introduces the simple notion of re-balancing. If leaders want to change the status quo of congregational life, they need to find ways to change the balance. They have to move the weights in order to prompt new action.

Re-balance inside programs

Congregations interested in equipping members to be Gospel-carriers may find the easiest place to begin is with existing programs. Shifting balance does not require adding new programs. Slight adjustments in existing programs can turn them inside-out. Adding a focus on neighbors may give new momentum to ongoing social ministry activities. Putting new weight on exercising gifts as good citizens might expand members' stewardship understanding. The easy part of re-balancing is making program adjustments. The harder part is learning to think differently, to consider God's mission from a worldly perspective. I usually begin by identifying real programs and activities typical in many congregations.

Consider evangelism, for example ...

When I'm teaching re-balancing to groups of church leaders, I ask them to list typical congregational evangelism activities. Any area of congregational life works, but evangelism is an easy one to use. As individuals suggest them, I jot down the activities on a large piece of newsprint.

The process is outlined below. Why not do it yourself while I describe the steps?

1. List some common activities in congregational evangelism programs.

A copy of the newsprint outline I use is on the next page. List some of the evangelism activities used in your church on the outline before reading further.

The lists groups devise usually include such items as greeters to welcome visitors, name tags, visitor-friendly bulletins, ads in the newspaper, flyers in mailboxes for Vacation Bible School, Invite-a-Neighbor Sundays, Wednesday worship in the summer, sponsors for new members, and letters and visits to first-time worshippers. Your list may include other items.

2. What do we mean when we use the term *evangelism*?

Once we form the activities list, I ask groups to define *evangelism*. Take a few moments to write your own definition here.

Groups take time to shake out their assumptions about evangelism. Sooner or later, someone goes to the word's root. The conversation shifts to talk of "bringing Good News," and ends up describing the objective of evangelism as sharing the Gospel.

3. Where do we share the Gospel?

Then, I redirect attention to the original newsprint list. Notice the two narrow columns that run down each margin. At the top, label the left column "in" and the right one "out".

Now, review your personal list.

■   Which activities are designed to bring people *inside* the church to hear the Gospel – even if they occur on the outside? Put check marks in the left-hand column for those items.

■   Which activities are designed to take the Gospel to people *outside* as a gift, not to win members? Put check marks for those activities in the right-hand column. Do this before reading further.

When I ask groups to sort activities into *inside* and *outside* columns, most – if not all – checks are placed in the left-hand column. This doesn't mean the evangelism activities listed are wrong. It just means that a lot of congregational evangelism programs are stuck in the *inside* position.

Evangelism in Our Congregation

INSIDE		OUTSIDE
	1.	
	2.	
	3.	
	4.	
	5.	
	6.	
	7.	
	8.	
	9.	
	10.	

4. How could we re-balance evangelism to place more attention outside?

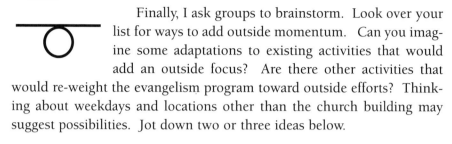

Finally, I ask groups to brainstorm. Look over your list for ways to add outside momentum. Can you imagine some adaptations to existing activities that would add an outside focus? Are there other activities that would re-weight the evangelism program toward outside efforts? Thinking about weekdays and locations other than the church building may suggest possibilities. Jot down two or three ideas below.

Groups find that slight alterations in the existing activities, or the addition of another activity, could re-balance programs on their lists. The "see-saw" of evangelism would gain momentum as it went back and forth, in and out.

One practical step to re-balancing existing programs is to look at them from an outside perspective.

Brainstorm simple, creative ideas.

Once they get the hang of it, group brainstorming will result in simple, creative ideas. As an example, take Invite-a-Neighbor Sunday. From the angle of "taking God's love outside," look at other days of the week and other locations. Some ideas:

1. Turn Invite-a Neighbor Sunday into a series of Sundays with special themes for both Sunday school and worship. This allows time for both discussing the theme and planning each week's actions, and for preaching and praying on the day's theme.

- The first Sunday might be "Thank Your Neighbor" Sunday, an opportunity to encourage members to show — during the next week — appreciation for the good they see in their neighbors.

- The next Sunday might be "Pray for Your Neighbor," tending during worship and Sunday school to the situations real neighbors are facing, and finding ways to share those concerns with God each day during the following week.

- "Serve Your Neighbor" Sunday might focus on asking members of all ages to find ways to help a neighbor during the coming week. These could be either anonymous or face-to-face.

Members would do something during the week that connects to their Sunday experience, paying attention to the same or different neighbors each week. On Sunday when members come *inside*, they would share their *outside* experiences and learn from each other. Finally, it would be time to ask neighbors to come to church.

2. "Invite Your Neighbor" Sunday could feature adult forums on community issues, collections of food for a local food bank, and craft projects children could complete and deliver to the nearest nursing home. Members who work in the neighborhood could be hosts.

Neighbors would be invited to church because the church was paying attention to their neighborhoods that Sunday. That's a twist on inviting neighbors in the hope that they will be attracted to the church. Instead, the church is demonstrating its attraction to the community, its residents and its workers. If that makes the congregation attractive to some neighbors, then great!

Vacation Bible School is another item from newsprint lists that groups often choose. They have suggested:

- Invite neighbors to participate in a community service project you will be doing. Note this on the VBS flyers used to invite them to attend the school.

- Sponsor a youth-run lemonade stand in a public spot, with contributions going to the town's day camp program.

- Conduct Bible school in a park pavilion on one day and the zoo on another.

Other ideas ...

In other words, take the Gospel story outside where people can see it, where they can eavesdrop or just watch from a park bench nearby. With the common interest of the community in mind, offer ways for outsiders to participate.

When groups start thinking about evangelism as a take-out idea, they come up with new ideas, too. They have suggested providing prayer cards for hospital patients who request them, conducting vespers monthly in the community room at the local mall, and distributing messages of appreciation to school teachers, hospital personnel and fire fighters at Thanksgiving. They have imagined members taking devotional booklets to neighbors, praying with co-workers, and reading Bible stories to children at family picnics.

Once, a person suggested handing out cups of water to participants in the local walkathon, prompting someone else to wonder about sharing pizza with youth in a juvenile detention facility. A third person suggested singing in public places, or at neighborhood street intersections, when the choir goes Christmas caroling. Once people start thinking about other places and days, they imagine all sorts of possibilities.

A church in Charlotte, North Carolina hosted a free car wash. Members, dressed as clowns, waved down cars and invited them into the church parking lot. Other members baked muffins to offer drivers while they waited for their cars. People were puzzled. Most of them tried to pay. "No," members responded, "it's free." I'm willing to bet that those drivers think about the Gospel message they experienced every time they drive by that church.

When groups see existing evangelism strategies from this new perspective, some of them conclude that a particular activity on the newsprint list is no longer appropriate. Or they come up with new activities. Occasionally, a group realizes that something they are doing now – such as hosting exchange students – has potential for carrying the Gospel outside. The more leaders talk, the fuzzier the lines between evangelism, worship, education and social ministry become.

But the more church-goers examine inside and outside perspectives, the clearer the connection between the church gathered and scattered becomes. Most of the things they are doing in the gathered community they will continue to do, some of them with a new twist. I call that turning a congregation inside-out.

These examples are rooted in ongoing congregational programs. Most of the activities would still happen inside, too, or at least find their impetus there. But church activities are more portable than they first appear to be. They can be taken to places where unchurched people work or play. Some can be done in partnership with the community – no strings attached. Church-goers have to develop the habit of thinking of seven days and other locations. Church activities nourish members of the gathered community. Those same activities can also encourage and equip members to be Gospel-carriers when they go their scattered ways.

Same steps, other uses

Using evangelism for re-balancing is not *the way* to turn congregations inside-out. Remember, it was used as an example. Possibilities for re-balancing can be found in other congregational programs, too. These steps can be used to review any part of the gathered community's life:

A. *List current activities.* What have we been doing in this area?

B. *Shake out assumptions.* What do we understand to be the purpose of this ministry?

C. *Check programs for balance.* Which activities are intended to draw people in? Which to send members out?

D. *Brainstorm to find twists on existing activities and suggest new ones.* Think both inside and outside. What could happen other days of the week in other locations? What would help members for their scattered daily ministries?

E. *Choose the most appealing possibilities.* Which ones will be easiest or make the most difference?

The questions may need some modification from program to program. But the basic process can be applied to any part of congregational life that seems to be stuck in an inside position.

Watch for opportunities …

Members participating in church programs will signal their need for help with this Gospel-carrying business. Give them many opportunities and then listen to the questions they ask. Demonstrate that their concerns are important or they will stop asking. Then be prepared to respond by altering or adding to existing plans.

During Lent last year, about 20 of us gathered each Wednesday evening for an excellent Bible study on Job. It was intellectually stimulating and produced interesting conversation. During the study, we examined the way Job's friends responded to his calamities. Each time we did that, several people would ask the same practical question: "What do we say to people we know who are suffering?" It was obvious that individuals had particular people and situations in mind. Some suggestions were offered in response, especially things *not* to say. Job's friends gave us plenty of examples, but the basic question remained, and it came up during each study session and the fellowship times that followed.

One of the reasons the question persisted was because a family in our congregation was suffering. A mother of two young boys was dying of cancer. Members were doing all they could think of for her, her husband and their sons. But what do you say, especially to the boys and to their young friends? Members were invited to a pizza supper so they could share their feelings, ask questions and receive some guidance for talking about death with children. While the impetus for the meeting came from the suffering of this one family, other situations and fears were shared, too. From beliefs that are central to our faith, we sorted out some of the awful things that are said about God and death. Individuals told stories about the loss of loved ones. People cried. Some of them came back a second time for a similar session. This time, the neighbors and parents of the boys' schoolmates were invited.

Adults appreciate scripture study that doesn't insult their intelligence. I believe this was the secret to the success of the Job study. They also want practical help about things that touch them emotionally. (It's the need to *practice* the faith again — in safe places.) Those in that Bible study really cared about people both known and unknown to our congregation. They were frustrated by their inability to respond to suffering. The study of Job focused their thinking. The pizza supper explored their role as Gospel-carriers.

Especially with youth …

Children and teenagers like to be taken seriously, too. But they don't have the leverage or voice in churches that adults have. Another practical approach to re-balancing might be to start with programs involving children and teenagers.

Start with programs involving children and teenagers.

The programs for younger members could be the easiest to turn inside-out. Not yet set in their ways, children are trying to find their way in the world. They have a special view of the church that is worth hearing. What is it like for a four-year-old to walk into the church building or a classroom filled with strangers for the first time? What is it like for that child to be in adult-oriented worship? Look at church with the eyes of a three-year-old. Invite children to share their impressions.

Jump a decade ahead and think about those children at 14. What kind of daily lives do those teenagers bring to church? What happens at church that speaks to being a teenager or shows respect for who they are? Adults bemoan the fact that young people leave the church. Perhaps congregations would understand this problem better if they looked at it from the youth's perspective. That would mean, of course, talking with and listening to teenagers. A good idea.

Think about the typical programs offered children and youth. How many crafty little projects using paper and crayons can one child do and still be excited? Where in congregational life do pre-teens have a chance to build their self-confidence? When do older teens have the undivided attention of any adults with whom it is safe to express their worries about grades, careers, sex or friends? Re-balance inside activities to equip young Christians to be Gospel-carriers:

1. Take youth to the food bank together with the cans of tuna fish they've collected, rather than delivering for them. They need to see what happens to their gifts outside the church.

2. Have Saturday lunch at the shopping mall food court with teenagers, listening to their feelings and learning about the pressures they face at home and school.

3. Help children and youth see the ministry they do daily, asking them what they did in class on Monday, after school on Wednesday or with others on Saturday. Listen for stories of things that happened, pointing out how they could or were sharing God's love in those situations.

4. Teach them that they are saints at times other than the first Sunday in November. I happened to be teaching young teens on one of those Sundays. They learned the lesson. Now when I see one of them, I often say "Hi, Saint Christie." She knows exactly what I mean.

5. Make it a practice to ask younger members about their public school classmates to see if any of them are sick or have problems. Include them in prayers. Help children plan things they can do to help playmates who are ill. Encourage teens to talk about friends with family problems; then in brainstorm sessions, seek ways to support those friends.

6. Ask people of various ages to lead worship. Many teenagers read scripture well. Children, who can help usher, understand the task and usually do it with big smiles. I've helped second graders compose prayers that were clear, appropriate petitions when offered later as the congregation gathered for worship.

7. Sing hymns that youth understand. One of our congregation's older youth observed that her little sisters "sort of lose it" when we sing hymns. Look at the selections your congregation sang in the last three months. How many have tunes Sunday school children know, use contemporary language and are easy to follow?

8. Go to soccer games and other competitive activities. Learn what the joys and frustrations are like for youth; then find the time and encourage them to talk about that after church on Sunday — perhaps while making ice cream sundaes in the fellowship hall.

9. Affirm their gifts as students, musicians, athletes, artists, scientists and model-makers. Some churches feature young people who play musical instruments. What about an exhibit of art or science fair

projects, giving time to discuss what those projects say about the world and the God who creates it? Consider publishing their poems and short stories in the church newsletter.

Consider other congregational activities ...

The same steps outlined on page 115 can be used in other ways. Follow them, for example, to assess the nature of the congregation's fellowship. What fosters a sense of community that draws members inside the church? What keeps that sense of community real to members when they are in their daily places?

Or, use the steps to plan for festivals or church year seasons. What activities draw members "inside" to observe Advent? What activities will help people observe Advent in their "outside" places? Think about the occasional worshippers who will come at Christmas and Easter. If they aren't going to come to church in-between times, what will stick with them during all those days outside? A token gift to put in their work places as a reminder of the Gospel news? Knowledge that they are being prayed for on a specific day every month? Being introduced to a member whose work days are similar, or one who works in the next office building?

Apply the process to different groups of members, too. What will bring the 20-somethings inside the church community more willingly? What encourages them to be faithful in their daily lives outside? How could the outside dimension of the church's life give new purpose to the ministry of members confined to their daily places by age or disability?

Re-balancing the vision of mission

The concept of re-balancing is easier to explain when demonstrating with examples of real programs. I started this chapter with some of those because I wanted to demonstrate that congregations can begin to turn themselves inside-out by making slight changes in existing activities. But just altering programs will not change attitudes or create a vision that propels congregations toward mission in the world. That takes re-balancing members' understanding and vision for God's mission for the church. That means reading both scripture and the world. (Chapter 3) It means shifting weights on the see-saw to bring the world in sight.

Meeting neighbors ...

In the first chapter, I contrasted two perspectives: those that clergy and lay members bring to the congregation. I acknowledged that I'd outlined oversimplified perspectives, and encouraged exploration of other insider views. I pointed out that members of different ages have different views. Now I want to take the matter of perspective another step: re-balancing vision by inviting neighbors to share views of both the church and their worlds.

Invite neighbors to share their views.

Gather members and neighbors who are representative of young families with children in your community. Or gather single professionals, grade school children, and widows and widowers. Invite groups by occupations, personal interests or around their geographic dwelling places. Explore the connections and dis-connections between their daily lives and organized religion.

Invite outsiders with different world perspectives. Talk to small business owners, police and bankers. Listen to community leaders and government officials. Converse with members and their assembly line co-workers. The whole truth about the church is learned from looking at it from many angles, both inside and outside.

Another good way to gain new perspectives on church is to go outside, literally. Walk the streets around city congregations; spend time in malls and grocery stores near suburban churches. Drive to stores and schools near rural churches. Visit the county seat. Talk to people along the way who can provide their own impressions of the church and its community.

Church-goers who do this will notice people they didn't expect to find as their neighbors. They may be upset by human need discovered in their church building's shadow, or surprised at the rich array of skills, creativity and knowledge demonstrated behind storefronts down the street. A basic step in re-balancing vision is discovering special opportunities churches have to deliver God's love wherever they are today.

Discover special opportunities churches have to deliver God's love wherever they are today.

One congregation may find that a shortage of neighborhood youth doesn't merit continuing to employ a part-time youth worker. Instead, they may discover that the number of older people with time on their hands suggests the need for a senior ministries coordinator. A congregation that thinks of itself as rural may discover that most members actually work in town, not on farms. God's mission for the church does not change, but often the context does. Congregations that get to know their parish neighbors begin to imagine new ways to announce the Gospel to people now living nearby.

The main point of this book is that lay members, who have information about the world, are Gospel-carriers into their daily places. Another step in re-balancing vision is to visually demonstrate this concept by re-drawing the congregation's boundaries to include its members' daily places.

Ask members to construct a pin map that includes both their home places (blue pins?) and work places (green pins?). Use the map to imagine ways to announce the Gospel to people in those scattered communities.

Re-draw the boundaries of the congregation to include the daily places of members.

Members who live at the junction of Routes 111 and 999 might be seeing a surge of apartment construction. New tenants will need community information, and some will be looking for services the church provides. Members who live along Elm Street might begin to notice youth congregating at the intersection with Park Avenue. Teen members might know what has prompted this new behavior. If a number of members are farmers, the congregation could ask what would carry God's love into the farming community. Areas of rural poverty might suggest one strategy, contaminated water run-offs another. If several members are teachers, the church could help them discern how to deliver God's love in classrooms where they are not allowed to talk about their Christian faith.

Later, it might be time to add yellow pins to show places where members volunteer. That could lead to another whole set of questions about how to do ministry in other parts of the community.

Pin maps visualize the places where congregations have the best opportunities to carry out their mission. They show places where the congregation has strength in numbers. Other devices, such as groups of workplace photographs on bulletin boards, could be used to demonstrate these re-drawn boundaries,. The important point is to find visual ways to help people recognize those places, and to imagine how God's love could bless people there.

Finding partners ...

When congregations begin to meet their neighbors, they will meet potential partners. Think about the partnerships churches can form with other congregations, social service agencies, schools and community organizations. Individual congregations become stronger when they learn to collaborate, rather than compete by duplicating efforts. This also frees resources that can be devoted to needs not being met by other churches or agencies. Another step in developing vision might be to build alliances with other groups that deliver God's love in the world. Recognize that God uses humanitarian, educational, government, business and religious institutions to do this.

Build alliances with other groups that deliver God's love in the world.

A strategy such as this allows smaller congregations to stretch their resources. But it can be valuable for larger congregations, too. Bigger congregations may be able to collaborate with community leaders by providing space needed by specific groups for programs and services. Several small congregations may be able to form an alliance with a university school of social work. I know of congregations in one city that provide building space for field offices used by a school during student internships.

Starting the mission ...

Think about your congregation's mission statement. How much of it is focused on what happens with members inside the church building? How much on what happens outside with others? Most of those I've read are inside documents. Some describe the character and ideals of the gathered community. Others outline congregational ministries – which may include being a welcoming, inviting community to outsiders. Few are outside documents that see the congregation as the "staging center" for going into the world.

What would happen to such mission statements if congregations redefined their mission as being both gathered and scattered? When congregations understand that ministry is not confined to church on Sundays, their mission vision widens. Members begin to see that they are in a position to carry out that mission wherever they are during the week.

When the mission statement is rewritten as an outside document, the daily ministry of members shows clearly as part of the congregation's mission. That statement should not be just printed and archived; its value grows as it provokes more conversation, and is reviewed and revised regularly.

Redefine the congregation's mission, gathered and scattered, and assess it regularly.

Imagine congregational meetings whose agendas reflect such mission statements. Standard reporting on inside activities has to make room for reports on outside ministries. Gospel-carrying members would have stories to tell of both joys and frustrations. Such meetings would take some getting used to, but they would be potentially more interesting than most of the ones I've attended.

Does changing the mission statement alter the mission of the church itself? No, the mission is changeless. Do these changes alter the church's ability to be about the mission? Yes, continually seeking to understand mission is at the heart of church renewal. The clearer this becomes, the freer churches are to adapt congregational models to serve that mission well.

No matter the size

A number of times in this book, I have said that congregations of any size can be channels for God's love. Any congregation can make better use of its resources in order to serve God's mission for the church. To grow in strength, it does not have to be a congregation growing in numbers. Congregations of any size become stronger as they grow in and practice faith more confidently. Mutual support and fellowship, well-made decisions, creativity and risk-taking are all strengths that don't come automatically with numerical and dollar increases. They can come both alongside or in spite of diminishing numbers and dollars.

Re-balancing programs and vision strengthens congregations, no matter their history or current circumstance. It helps them use their current gifts and resources now, rather than waiting until they are better off.

Program that fits now ...

Whatever their resources, congregations control the programs they offer. They decide what issues they wish to address, and whose needs they wish to meet. They do not have to offer every program that nearby congregations offer. In fact, it might be smart to concentrate on real issues and needs *not* being addressed elsewhere.

Programs ought to fit congregations as they are; they should be "do-able" under present conditions. If the current facilities do not include a gym, the idea of a senior high volleyball league doesn't fit *unless* there is an available gym nearby and the funds to rent it. If there is no staff person specializing in geriatrics, then a support group for adults dealing with aged parents *only fits* if there is a specialist available who would lead the group for a modest stipend. If Sunday school classrooms are overcrowded and there's no room to expand, adding a parents' program at the same time doesn't fit, *unless* the restaurant down the block will set out a continental breakfast and let you use their private dining room.

Look inside and outside for resources that may be less obvious, but are already available now.

Adding program *does not* necessarily mean adding staff and space. There may be other options. If a new program really supports mission, a re-balancing strategy is to look inside and outside for less-obvious resources that are available *now*. Don't wait for more staff, space or money. Sometimes, looking from another angle, you find creative answers.

Adding program *does* mean spending existing resources differently. Congregations grow stronger when they make wise choices with the resources they have, rather than spending down resources that are too thin.

A central vision …

Congregations that are guided by a central vision have a good basis for making decisions. They are not like status-quo congregations that keep the same programs going from year to year, no matter what the changes in needs or situations. They are not trapped by decisions based on traditions that have turned into habits.

Because these congregations have talked about their vision over and over again, the image of mission in the pastor's head looks like the images in the minds of lay leaders. That is one of their strengths. Their decisions, therefore, are not based on tradition or novelty, but on mission goals. They can be selective in programming, and their sense of mission guides them in choosing to begin, continue, change or end programs.

The end result of mission-aimed programming is that members are nourished in their faith, and the Gospel is demonstrated to outsiders. If programs do not nourish members in ways that help further the mission, are they worthy ways to use resources? Is that good stewardship? If programs don't help outsiders see the Gospel, what purpose do they serve?

Use a clear, central vision to make the most of the congregation's resources.

When churches can make decisions based on a common, shared mission, they can also make decisions on the best ways to use their resources in support of mission. They can talk about the programs on which their pastors need to spend time, and the ones lay members have the gifts to lead. They can re-assign building space and budget dollars. Congregations re-balance themselves when they use a clear, central vision to make the most of the resources they have.

Chapter 7

Shift the direction

"How could we do things differently *inside* to better carry God's love *outside*?" Congregations can be turned inside-out *by making simple, attractive changes that will, over time, alter the congregation's direction.* The last chapter offered one practical approach: change programs and mission statements by re-balancing them with a view toward the outside world. This final chapter offers a second practical answer: change the culture, values and relationships within the congregation by making slight shifts in ongoing church life patterns. Any church – no matter its situation – can do this.

Congregations will stay on paths they have been following for years until something pulls them in another direction. How do we insiders cultivate a climate for change among members who take comfort in the church's stability and predictability? We need to engage them in experiences that are satisfying and beneficial, ones that someday will give them pause to re-consider what it means to be the church.

Kirken Kin

Our Pennsylvania congregation was one of those "hour glass" communities. There were a number of the longtime, faithful who had stayed through thick and thin, not many middle-age members or families with teenagers, and a growing number of young families with small children. One mother, new to the congregation, described what it was like to bring her 3-year-old to worship alone. Another mother, whose children always had Grandpa waiting in the pew to make them feel welcome, empathized.

From that brief conversation came an idea. A dozen three-year-olds were starting Sunday school that fall. Why not ask their parents if they would like the children to have a church grandparent; we called them "Kirken

Kin", to avoid confusion with real grandparents. Parents liked the idea. So did the members we asked to fill the grand-parenting role. All they had to do was exchange photos and pay attention to one child on Sunday morning.

Of course, they did much more. It was wonderful to watch. There were cards on birthdays and little Christmas gifts. Not only were Kirken Kin seen with "their" children beside them at worship, they were also sighted with them at McDonald's and the miniature golf course. Kirken Kin were invited to picnics and other family activities. Grandma Patsy brought Julie to church to help her prepare the altar for Sunday. Leeann was heard running down the center aisle of the nave after worship one Sunday calling "Where's Aunt Jane? Where's Aunt Jane?" She was carrying the cake she had baked for her Kirken Kin's birthday.

Then we noticed something even more wonderful. Table groups during our after-worship fellowship time were transformed. No longer were longtime members clustered together while new members sat at other tables. The parents of the young children and the longtime members were talking to each other, building relationships of their own. That simple idea changed the culture of our congregation.

Simple, appealing actions open the door to change. In this case, longtime members agreed that young children should have familiar, friendly faces to welcome them when they come to church. Everyone saw value in the idea. The grandparent connection was a non-threatening way to link members from two generations. The Kirken Kin idea didn't change everything in our congregation, but it unsettled the status quo in a wonderful way. Because it built a new network of relationships, later changes were easier instead of harder.

Simple, not easy ...

There is no easy way to change everything in congregations quickly – at least none that I've witnessed. It's difficult to reshape a congregation's culture. A whole new set of leaders may take charge but may still operate as leaders did two generations back. I've seen this pattern in real congregations and watched congregational leadership teams struggle with change in simulated situations. Even in the fictitious congregations, with the option to move in agreed-upon preferable directions, teams still find it hard to change paths. Loyalty may get in the way, or a sense of obligation, or a fear of lost identity. Inertia works against change, too. Accommodating the status quo seems easier than figuring out a new way to operate.

Given resistance to change, it would be naive to suggest that dramatic changes will happen in congregations except, perhaps, out of painful crises. But I'm not willing to give in to the status quo. I believe we can initiate some actions that will, over time, change congregations. The approach I'm suggesting in this chapter requires creativity, patience and persistence. Dramatic change is a slim possibility, but turning congregations more clearly toward mission is a viable option. This approach is workable in any size congregation, no matter its history or current circumstance.

Trim tabs

Peter Senge, director of the Center for Organizational Learning at the Massachusetts Institute of Technology's Sloan School of Management, describes the principle of leverage in *The Fifth Discipline*. He contends that "small, well-focused actions can sometimes produce significant, enduring improvements if they're in the right place."[10]

Senge uses a Buckminster Fuller illustration to explain the concept of leverage.

> *A trim tab is a small "rudder on the rudder" of a ship. It is only a fraction the size of the rudder. Its function is to make it easier to turn the rudder, which, then, makes it easier to turn the ship. The larger the ship, the more important is the trim tab because a large volume of water flowing around the rudder can make it difficult to turn.*[11]

Trim tabs are *not obvious* to the casual observer, nor do they require great effort to operate. However, they produce a significant result as they relieve pressure to pull the ship in the desired direction.

Our Pennsylvania congregation did not know it at the time, but Kirken Kin became the appealing trim tab that pulled different parts of our congregation together. It was a small, well-focused action that encouraged change in our community and was sustained by the relationships it formed among members.

Simple, not easy ...

Congregations often put planning committees in charge of renewal or growth. These committees may work through strategic planning on their own, with a consultant, or by following advice offered by one of the many entrepreneurs who write books and conduct seminars.

The committees survey the congregation, set goals and assign responsibilities. Sometimes this works fairly well. But many times planning begins with great fanfare and by implementing a few actions, only to settle back into a slightly-altered version of the status quo. It takes a lot of energy and persistence to generate significant change within congregations. Rather than "Apply the trim tab," the motto is more likely to be "Don't rock the boat."

If a congregation needs to shift direction to be truer to its mission, the trim tab idea offers an alternative to a major planning process. It's certainly less complicated and much faster to put into place, but it isn't a quick-fix. Trim tabs usually don't produce big changes rapidly. Remember, however, that just a little leverage on the rudder alters the course of the big ship. The change is hardly noticeable at the time the trim tab is applied, but later, miles away, it will make a big difference.

Trim tabs are not clever ways to manipulate congregations into doing things members don't want. That requires power plays or heavy-handed *pushing*. Trim tabs attract members; they work by *pulling*, by relieving pressure. Their immediate impact is negligible, but months later members may notice changes in relationships or accept new values.

Consider the qualities of these small, well-focused actions that produce significant, enduring improvements.

- ■ Trim tabs are not obvious. This doesn't mean that they are hidden or secret. They just do not attract inordinate attention or cause much debate. Their purposes seem clear and the results valuable. Although our congregational newsletter reported on the Kirken Kin idea and invited participation, the activity was barely noticeable to the membership majority.

- ■ Trim tabs do not require great effort; they are low energy. They don't divert a lot of resources (time or money), but do require some creativity which can be invigorating. The demands on Kirken Kin were minimal. Those who were interested invested more of themselves because they were enjoying new relationships. The connection was made at church but spilled over into daily places.

■ Trim tabs relieve pressure. The real secret to a ship's trim tab is that it lessens the water pressure against the ship, allowing it to move in the desired direction. Instead of pushing the congregation into making a hard change, trim-tab actions pull people along. The action is an attractive one that people welcome. The Kirken Kin notion was appealing to members who had no children of their own, or whose grandchildren lived far away. They were glad to be asked.

The best trim tab actions are sustainable ones that can provide continuing leverage for change. Think of them not as one-shot actions, but as initiating ongoing practices that pull congregations toward the church's mission.

Trim tabs can make improvements in congregations of any size. They can open up the culture and norms of both old and new congregations, but they are custom-made. Kirken Kin was the right action at the right time for our congregation. That doesn't mean it would have the same benefits for other congregations. It wasn't our only creative idea — we tried many things to improve the congregation's climate — yet only in hindsight did we realize how significant was this simple action.

I have no magic list of eight trim tabs that are guaranteed to turn congregations inside-out, but I have defined their measurements. Test your ideas against the three descriptions above. If they are very obvious, require great effort, or add pressure they are not trim tabs. If they can be revamped to be less obvious — more effortless and un-pressured — they might turn into trim tabs. Most of all, test the hoped-for results of these ideas against the congregation's mission-direction. Will the trim tab turn the church in the right direction?

While I cannot package trim tabs that will turn congregations inside-out, I can suggest four possibilities. Three come from congregations who have been modeling this book's ideas for several years. The last is one I've been suggesting throughout the book. Consider trim tab possibilities around prayer, church newsletters, the daily places of members and scripture.

Loud-praying members

At first glance, prayer seems a strange choice for leveraging directional change in congregations, but take a second look. Prayer is an appealing part of congregational life that needs no introduction. Would members resist putting more emphasis on prayer? Hardly; even people who are not church-goers value prayer. Since it attracts people, prayer is a natural source for trim tabs.

Prayer defines congregations, too. Who prays — and what they pray about — speaks volumes concerning a congregation's sense of mission. Think about it. Who, besides the pastor, prays out loud at your church? Perhaps other staff, teachers in their classes, and little children before they are old enough to be embarrassed. Why is it that members can't go through the potluck buffet line until their pastors have finished greeting worshippers, taken off their vestments, and made it to fellowship hall? Is it because part of the pastor's job is to pray or because members defer to the pastor's training and authority? Think of the message conveyed if pastors are the only people seen praying when the congregation gathers.

Consider the content of prayers prayed in your church. Where do they set the boundaries for the church's mission? Is there balance between petitions for church and world leaders — local and global — and between church activities and community events? Are the prayers for the sick and bereaved centered on members or do they include neighbors, colleagues and distant relatives? Congregations who are in ministry seven days a week in different places will have neighborhoods, ball parks and 4-H clubs to pray for, and cooks, locksmiths, 6th graders and corporate vice presidents to pray about.

Prayer content always shows what is important and acceptable in congregations; it is a telling indicator of the church's direction. Changes in prayer practices can be made with little effort and without calling inordinate attention to them. Indeed, this may be a good way to begin turning congregations inside-out.

Gospel-carriers are Christians who are able to pray for and with others when they are outside of the church building. Trim tabs that encourage them to pray aloud with other members inside church give them practice for praying outside. Trim tabs that expand prayer petitions to include outside concerns tell both church-goers and visiting worshippers that the congregation cares about delivering God's love to the world. Consider these ideas from some real congregations:

■ **Pray for specific members and have a prayer workshop.** Several members and the pastor of one congregation proposed this trim-tab action: They placed a prayer tree in the narthex, with cards containing names of all members tied to its branches. As worshippers left Sunday worship, they would take one card and, during the coming week, pray for the person named on it. The congregation liked the idea – it had *pull* to it. But there was an obstacle – a number of people said they really didn't know how to pray. That led to a prayer workshop that was well-attended by members of all ages. The congregation worked on learning to pray, and began to use the prayer tree.

■ **All members pray about the same issue for a week.** A second congregation hands out business-size prayer cards each Sunday. They contain a Bible verse and a focus for the week on which the whole congregation will concentrate prayers. Sometimes the focus is a church concern, but most weeks it is outside — on matters of ethics, government, environment and society. Members are encouraged to place the cards where they will see them daily —on refrigerators, office desks or in their pockets.

■ **Members pray without ceasing some days.** In another congregation, life-threatening surgery facing one member offered an opportunity. Members signed up for 30-minute periods during which they promised to pray for Cynthia on her surgery day. Many of them gathered at church early that morning for prayer, and the pastor provided suggestions and formats for their private prayer times that day.

Later, one mother reported that she had explained the importance of her prayer time to her two pre-schoolers. She was amazed at how they quietly honored her need for uninterrupted time. She also prayed longer than her allotted time – just in case the next person was delayed. People prayed at church, work and home throughout the day. That crisis opportunity established a new pattern for congregational praying. This practice could be used for major decisions facing the congregation, in the wake of national tragedies, or on special occasions such as the start of the school year.

■ **Members share prayer concerns during worship.** In a fourth congregation, the prayers at worship are preceded by conversation as the pastor moves through the congregation. Individuals suggest petitions they would like to have included. While illnesses are mentioned frequently, other concerns are shared, too: neighbors in the throes of divorce, changes in job situations, troops headed to foreign places, community, national or global issues. Reasons for joy and prayers of thanksgiving are also shared as a child raises her hand to say it's her mom's birthday next week, or a couple announces they are expecting twins. Someone may ask for blessings on a family reunion, or a good year at college.

By the way they describe each situation, members actually formulate the petitions. The pastor just helps put them into words. It's more comfortable than the silence that often greets a pastor who asks people to offer their own petitions. The pastor doesn't try to repeat the details of each prayer request, but gathers them in a few general petitions interspersed with moments of silence. The praying really began earlier — when the first person raised her hand to say her sister had been diagnosed with breast cancer.

■ **Prayer boxes are reminders in daily places.** The pastors of a California congregation preached a series of sermons addressing Baptism and the parables on salt, yeast and light. Each Sunday, they gave members tokens by which to remember the sermons: a sea shell, packets of salt and yeast, a votive candle. They gave members little plastic boxes in which to place these tokens and a workplace prayer. Those boxes can be found on office desks and kitchen counters, in plumbers' trucks, behind display cases in retail stores, and at nursing stations. They are reminders to pray and conversation starters with co-workers. Members of other congregations use mission statements pinned to bulletin boards, or have placed other symbols there that remind them of their baptismal calling as they go about their daily work.

Though little children are uninhibited and direct in their prayers, they lose that simplicity as they grow older. They need to see older children, teenagers and adults praying. They need to hear prayers before meals, during meetings, in the homes of sick friends, at sundown on the beach and after angry words have been spoken. Congregations model prayer behavior at church that carries over into daily life. The richer the model, the more prayers will spill over into workplaces and neighborhoods.

Appealing church newsletters

A second area with potential for shifting direction is the newsletter. This, too, seems a strange choice at first glance. Unlike prayer, it is not so highly valued. Some members do not even read the newsletter, and some newsletters are not very readable. But like prayer, newsletters are a feature of congregational life. Their content has a role in shaping the congregation's values and vision.

Adding articles about outside issues — time and again — would shift attention toward a mission of delivering God's love to the world. Members need to hear about specific situations and receive practical suggestions that encourage them to deliver God's love on the outside.

Having read newsletters from many congregations, I think it's safe to say that many are pieced together the same way every year, with little thought to format, content or how the overall message is conveyed. With some revamping, they can be excellent vehicles for telling how God's love is delivered in the world.

Congregational newsletters will be interesting artifacts for future generations to study. Look at some past issues of yours. What might readers 100 years hence conclude about your congregation's mission, or learn about issues facing members in the early 21st century? Would the things reported give readers an accurate impression of what is important to your church?

When you look at your newsletters, try to read them from the perspective of a member who attends only occasionally. What message do you receive? What parts will interest you if you are not able to worship often, or do not belong to any groups that meet regularly? Does the newsletter tell you what is happening with fellow members or others for whom you might be praying? How does it bolster tenuous ties to less involved members?

Now, imagine that you are an outsider who picked up this newsletter in a dentist's office. What would you learn about the purpose and activities of the congregation? What attitudes are conveyed about those who are not members? Is there anything that might make your congregation attractive to the dentist's patients?

If mission is directed into the world and members minister in daily life, that should be visible in church newsletters. Modest, unobtrusive alterations in newsletters could open up a new vision for mission. For example:

- ■ **Call attention to community activities.** The newsletter of one congregation regularly promotes activities planned by other religious and civic groups. The column, *Invitations from Neighbors*, faces the church calendar. The events are listed on the appropriate day of the calendar and cross-referenced in the column. The newsletter also runs articles by members who outline emerging community issues and opportunities for volunteer service.

- ■ **List inside & outside prayer petitions.** The worship committee in another congregation realized that only members who were in church on Sunday would know who was prayed for, and why. Listing names in the newsletter — even though the information would not always be up-to-date — not only kept all members informed, but started a conversation about other appropriate prayer concerns to list. Eventually, a feature called *The Petition Box* was added. It contained prayer requests for members and non-members, church and global issues, birthdays and baptismal anniversaries, different occupations each month, and seasonal gifts of God.

- ■ **Highlight inside activity with outside impact.** A Minnesota congregation, working hard to turn itself inside-out, has developed a logo that symbolizes their understanding of the ministry of the baptized in their daily places. Members recognize the logo. It appears beside any newsletter article that promotes or exemplifies the concept. Month-by-month, members are reminded how their congregation delivers God's love into the world.

- ■ **Do outside "thank yous," too.** That same congregation does a *Thank You* column each month. Formerly restricted to things members and non-members did inside the congregation, it now thanks members and non-members for things they are doing in the community and at work. This sends a different message to readers, doesn't it?

■ **Interview members.** Another congregation interviews members, including children and teenagers, about their daily ministries. A young journalist member writes monthly articles based on the interviews. Here is the approach Barbara uses, asking the same four questions of three people for each article.

1. **Have you always been a member of this church?**
   This starts people talking. Sometimes a spouse brought them, or this was most like their childhood congregation. Some have always been members of the same denomination, others come because it is close to home or their best school friends belong.

2. **Who were/are your mentors?**
   Some will mention friends, relatives, a pastor, co-worker or teacher. They will share stories about the influence of these mentors.

3. **What are your gifts?**
   People need prompting on this one. You may need to suggest gifts you've observed them using, or ask what they enjoy doing or interests them. Youth may want to talk about what they enjoy in school or hope to do later in life.

4. **What is your ministry in daily life?**
   If this draws a blank at first, pose it in ways that may prompt a response. For instance, "How do you take your faith to work? Do you talk about your faith at work or school? How has your example as a Christian influenced your co-workers or class-mates? When do people seek you out for advice? How does God help you in these situations? Do you pray for these people?"

These articles are gentle, safe ways for members to witness to one another. The spotlight is always on their lives as Christians in the world, with some allusion to ways they participate in the congregation. Imagine reading such articles. Not only would you know fellow members better, you would know many more ways people can minister in daily places. You would be getting the message that all members minister — and they do it both inside and outside the church.

Church newsletters will be read more often by more members if they are well-formatted and have interesting content. The time and energy it might take to put it in good shape makes it sound like more than a trim tab, but it may be worth the effort. With a good design in place, production time and energy would be about the same as before. If revamping the whole newsletter seems daunting, try re-formatting one page to carry certain monthly features or recruit writers to do particular columns. Some homebound members with writing skills or good community contacts might be glad to spend their spare time doing this.

Newsletters are not the only print communication tools available to congregations. Think about Sunday bulletins and bulletin boards which may also be used to shape values and set directions.

Frequented daily places

While most "well-focused actions" will occur inside congregations, a few trim tabs could occur in outside places, also.

There are many ways to take the church outside. Program ideas in the previous chapter suggest outside locations. The section on *Meeting neighbors* (Chapter 6) includes trim tab possibilities. The trim tab actions congregations have suggested to me, however, focus on members' daily work places.

It's clear that spotlighting work places as mission locations could shift the direction of the congregation and turn it inside-out. While some of that can happen from inside the church, what not-so-obvious, easy and appealing actions can the church initiate on the outside? Here are both inside and outside possibilities:

■ **The "HELP" bulletin board.** One congregation sets up a special bulletin board at the fellowship hall entrance. Members place "ads" here when they need practical, job-related help. For example, a social worker was overwhelmed with the number of "negligent" parents in his case load. Parenting classes had provided help for some of them. His note sought people interested in mentoring parents of first graders. Three members eventually became the nucleus of a support team that coaches parents and children weekly. A fast-food manager member had an employee whose minimum-wage earnings could not provide adequate clothing for her three-year-old. He listed needed clothes, and placed a small box below the board. It was overflowing in a week. One or two of these ads are printed in the Sunday bulletin weekly, also. More eyes will see them there, and this reminds people that offerings, other than ones in the collection plate, are needed, too.

■ **Ministry to care-givers.** Joyce, a dialysis nurse, chaired our congregation's worship committee. When the committee planned a healing service for home-bound members, Joyce said that she wished her dialysis patients could come, too. Well, why not? Thanks to our para-transit system, transportation was not hard to work out. The service was well attended, as members who help members with disabilities also lent a hand to the dialysis patients.

Doctors and nurses from the hospital's dialysis unit also came. One of them observed that they had no place to put their grief when patients grew weak or died from lacking a transplanted organ. This congregation had found a way to invite them inside. It gave them a place to be medical professionals expressing their faith ecumenically. This was not a strategy to win new members, but an opportunity to share God's love with both patients and caregivers.

■ **Another ministry to caregivers.** Half a continent away, a congregation thought about a different set of care givers. Planning a special dinner and worship service for shut-ins, they began to think about all the people who care for shut-ins daily. Family members joined neighbors, nurses, Meals-On-Wheels drivers and others in the care system. Plans for honoring these care givers took shape.

■ **Maps and networks.** I know several congregations who find ways to show the daily places of members visually. Some use pin maps (described in Chapter 6). Others create bubble maps on large sheets of newsprint taped to their fellowship room walls. Each sheet identifies clusters of occupations, such as education, sales, construction, health care, school, home, etc. Members "sign in" on the newsprint that represents their daily place. This is an excellent way to collect information about work places and builds support systems centered on occupations. One congregation makes it a feature of the annual congregational meeting.

■ **Workplace blessings.** One congregation was accustomed to its pastors conducting house blessings when members moved into new homes. During Epiphany, the pastors asked if any members would like their workplaces blessed, also. They did. One member, a watch commander in the county prison, asked for the blessing because he "wanted all the help he could get." The pastor met the watch commander in his office, talked about his work and prayed. Then they toured the prison while silently praying that this place could be claimed by God's presence. They did not interrupt the work of others, but they did meet co-workers who were interested in the fact that the man's pastor was there.

That same pastor visited a member who entered price codes into the computer system of a local grocery store. With permission, she told her co-workers and they offered suggestions for prayers they wanted offered. Employees continued at their tasks, but were aware that when the pastor and their co-worker were at the checkout counter a prayer was being offered about prejudice against customers using food stamps. When the two went to the parking lot, they offered a prayer for safety, especially in the hours from dusk to dawn.

■ **New member sponsors.** One congregation has gone another step with member sponsorship of new members. Trying to match people within occupational groupings, the pastor asks that sponsors make a point of visiting the newcomers' work places and invite them to visit their own daily work sites. This can happen either during or after working hours. Occasionally, it means breakfast in a nearby diner, or fast food on a building site. The pastor encourages members to continue this on a regular basis. Sometimes, he suggests others in the same occupation with whom they might also like to share a meal. It's the start of occupational support groups.

■ **Practicing the faith at soccer games.** Most of the church conversations I've heard about hockey and soccer schedules are critical of parents who let games interfere with Sunday school. But in one congregation, the pastors sat with soccer moms and dads to talk about alternative ways to do Christian education, and opportunities for worship that didn't make families have to choose one or the other. It certainly was a conversation welcomed by the parents. In this congregation, it led to equipping parents to do home-based education, sometimes with two or three families meeting together to share the responsibility.

The meetings with parents started interesting conversations about being Christian on the sidelines. The pastors asked parents to consider the other adults they met during these games. What were they hearing from these people? How could they help parents who were pushing their children too hard, or not managing their tempers well? These parents became both more involved in their children's Christian education and discovered very practical ways to be the church on public athletic fields.

Thinking about workplaces tends to bring to mind places where "grown-ups" spend their time. But children and youth have work places, too. Those include athletic fields. How does the church support people in their play places? What kind of visits could pastors make to schools that would bless those places for member students? Youth frequent places other than schools and playing fields during the week. There must be ways to demonstrate that the church understands and cares about them when they are in all of those places.

Bible-applying scholars

The last area I want to suggest that may have trim tab potential is Bible study. I do this more from hope than from experience. My list of stories will be short, but I firmly believe that when Christians learn to use scripture as a resource for daily living it changes both their outside daily lives and their inside church lives. Many lay people have a love-fear relationship with the Bible. They are certainly attracted to it. They cite favorite passages and willingly listen to sermons preached about it. However, they are afraid that they do not know it well because they can't quote scripture or find certain references quickly.

The Bible is a hard book. Church-goers need practice in finding their way around in the Bible. They need to be able to find particular books, chapters and verses. They need good Bibles to work with. How do they choose from the plethora of translations available? I find that Bible margin notes are often more of a problem than the translations themselves, and note that many church-goers have never seen a Bible commentary or concordance.

People look for ways to locate passages appropriate to concerns they bring to their Bible reading. What might comfort them when a loved one dies, when facing an unethical employer, or hearts brim with joy? If they used the Bible in church frequently, talked about and helped each other find scripture that spoke to daily issues, they would become familiar with the Bible and more confident in their ability to use it on their own.

Think about ways members use the Bible inside your congregation. Do they hear readings from an actual Bible, or from Sunday school storybooks and worship folders? I recall a 6th grader telling me that as a child she didn't realize that the stories she heard in Sunday school came from the Bible. She didn't make the connection until her mother picked up the Bible and read the same stories to her at home. That's an important insight. Storybooks are fine alongside the Bible and worship folders are helpful, but seeing the lector read the passage from the Bible itself makes a visual impression.

Perhaps pastors need to regularly ask members to read psalms from pew Bibles each Sunday, or occasionally locate scripture passages during sermons. This is an example of the scripture-to-life approach with which church-going members are most familiar. There is also the life-to-scripture approach, recognizing life situations and responding to them with God's Word. For example: begin monthly council meetings by scanning the local newspaper to see what is going on in the world, looking for scripture that speaks to those issues. Both approaches are valuable, and Gospel-carrying Christians need to be skilled at both.

- ■ **Read daily life epistles.** A pastor I know asks members to write their own epistle lessons, basing them on their daily work situations and issues they face. After each article is written, the pastor and member meet to talk about it. The member then reads the story to the congregation as another lesson during worship on an upcoming Sunday. The pastor's sermon relates the Gospel for that Sunday to the member's epistle.

- ■ **Practice with pericopes.** In our congregation, a group of adults meets each Sunday morning for coffee and conversation. Topics vary, but during Epiphany last year the following routine was used effectively. The session began with these questions: "What was happening in your life last week? "What was God revealing to you in those situations?" The responses grew richer from week to week. Then the group read the Gospel pericope (lesson) appointed for that Sunday. It was studied for its own merit and meaning. The last part of the session was devoted to see if – and how – the Gospel spoke to the situations shared at the start of the session.

■ **Bible sponsors.** Another congregation is considering asking adult members to present child members age-appropriate Bibles or story-books. If able, the adults would contribute to the purchase of the Bibles, inscribe, wrap and give them to the children on a specific Sunday morning. There might be a breakfast or lunch to celebrate the occasion. A team formed by the adult, a child, and his or her parents, would then learn to use the Bible, and help each other practice daily Bible reading. This would help the children, give them special attention, and perhaps help some adults learn their way around the Bible, also.

Loud-praying members, appealing newsletters, frequented daily places and Bible-applying scholars – these start a list of sources for trim tabs. Add to it.

Doing church differently

The persistent question throughout this book has been "How could we do things differently inside to better carry God's love outside?" If we church-goers feel any urgency about bringing Good News and healing into God's loved world, we need to prepare ourselves to do that in church. That is the one place where we are in charge. While we have little ability to influence the outside world directly, we do have power to touch with God's love people living out there. Eventually, that could make a difference in the world.

We have power to change ways of thinking, establish different relationships, install new decision-making habits, re-allocate resources, and choose values we wish to keep or replace. These are manageable, practical steps that we can take to advance God's mission.

We can do this in large and small congregations, in both overly-dependent and innovative ones. That doesn't mean change in the church is easy. It does mean it is possible.

We know that Christians need to congregate. The nurture of the gathered community is precious. Nothing in this book is intended to minimize the importance of congregational life. Most of what happens in churches now is good and should continue. Some of it needs to turn in the direction of God's loved world.

We need to live our lives as a gathered community thoughtfully, with the Bible and the world in mind. We cannot be satisfied with our congregations if they become ends in themselves. That is not a measure of success. Serving God, together and separately, is what counts.

Recognize and respect the fact that pastors and lay members see their congregations from different places.

Welcome differences and harness the energy tension produces.

Seek out God's perspective.

Re-consider assumptions about "church" and "mission" long taken-for-granted.

Take the ministry of both clergy and laity seriously.

Give equal attention, in church programs and mission statements, to carrying the Gospel to everyday, outside places.

Make simple, attractive changes that will, over time, change the congregation's direction.

I keep looking for ways the gathered community of believers could help members be the church, even when they are scattered in the world. The early church did it by coming together to celebrate what God was doing in the world and their lives. They learned from each other and exchanged ideas. They taught each other how to talk about faith so they could share it with others. The gathered community was a place of help and healing for those who suffered. It offered time for retreat and refreshment before members scattered to their separate, daily places.

Our circumstances are certainly different from those first Christian communities. Our North American society has moved away from religious values to secular ones. Christians are more likely to be met with indifference today than with the outright hostility of the 1st century.

Today's congregations don't have the flexibility of those early Christian gatherings. We have bills to pay and denominational guidelines to follow. Pastors are expected to build strong congregations with growing memberships and bank accounts. Is there any room in our church systems — local or denominational — to take a different approach? Where will pastors find support for shaking loose old habits and stale values?

Like Jesus' first generation followers, lay people today come in all sizes and conditions, with an endless variety of gifts and limitations. Some are strong and sure in their faith, others are timid or seasonal. They bear a strong resemblance to the recruits Jesus sent out to proclaim and heal. Will the church trust lay people to carry the Gospel into the indifferent world of this new century? Or will it see them as contented, dependent sheep?

"How could we do things differently inside to better carry God's love outside?" We can behave as though we expect church-goers to be Gospel-carriers. We can equip and encourage them in their calling. The rhythms of life in early communities of believers are instructive. Some of their patterns of coming and going, learning, failing and trying again, continue to make sense.

It is still the world God loves. It is into the world that God calls church-goers to carry Good News and healing. The gathered community (church) is there so we can return to tell what happened, and through it gain the courage to go back and try again.

End notes

10 Senge, Peter. *The Fifth Discipline*. Currency Doubleday. New York, New York. 1990. p.64

11 Ibid.

Postlude:

Witnesses to the wind of God

Who has seen the wind? Neither you nor I. But when the trees bow down their heads. The wind is passing by.[12]

Wind, tongues of fire, speaking in other languages — Luke's description of Pentecost is so amazing, and yet can be dulled by familiarity. Not so for those who gathered to worship at Holy Trinity Lutheran Church, Wallingford, Pennsylvania on Pentecost, 2001. The Spirit's wind was in their midst. They witnessed God's power — without a public word being spoken — through the language of daily work.

God's wind blew through Holy Trinity that Sunday. People who came filled with anticipation found good cause to rejoice, those who became frightened were aided and comforted, and those who felt helpless kept praying and singing. "The Spirit of God is like the wind," the pastor preached, "Recognize God's presence in the actions of people around you."

The sermon ended, Mike and Josh came to the altar to affirm their baptism, profess their faith and make their confirmation promises. As the congregation sang a hymn, ever so slowly members became aware of a medical emergency. Grant was to receive communion for the first time on this Pentecost. His grandparents had come to share that special moment, and now Grant's grandfather was stretched out on a pew.

Within moments, the worshippers took action. David, a paramedic new to the congregation, talked calmly with the family. Lilian, a chiropractor, knelt in the aisle cradling the grandfather's head. Cynthia and Marvelene, both nurses, bent over the pew to assist. Larry, a volunteer fire-rescue squad member, waited outside for the ambulance. Others sought to lend support to family members or to gather up Nicholas, Lilian's young son.

The congregation continued worship. The president acknowledged the two confirmands and offered them encouraging words. The paramedic team came up the aisle. Their questions and the responses concerning medications and medical history provided an antiphonal cadence to the choir's anthem. As they checked vital signs, members gave their offerings, prayed The Prayers and exchanged The Peace. While the congregation sang "Holy, Holy, Holy... Lord God of power and might," Grant's grandfather received an IV. As Larry, back in his role as an usher, directed people forward for communion, the grandfather was stabilized, placed on a stretcher and taken to the ambulance. Grant, with his mother and younger sister, was at the altar receiving the bread and wine.

Sunday is a time when Christians gather for worship. The worship liturgy is often defined as "the work of the people." At Holy Trinity that Pentecost, the worship work of the people happened alongside some of the members' Monday work. People in the medical field who had come to worship suddenly found themselves applying skills they use the rest of the week. While most of the congregation knelt at the altar, a few who could help knelt beside Grant's grandfather. Worship and daily ministry were intertwined.

If we could remember this Pentecost scene at each Sunday's worship, we'd be reminded that the people congregated around us have been on their knees literally or figuratively all week long. They are fixing plumbing, planting seed, tying shoes, teaching children, selling computers, poring over financial records, running businesses or looking for jobs. It would help us understand how demanding and tiring ministry in daily life can be, and how necessary worship is to restore and strengthen us all. Worship is our Sunday way to praise God.

If we could remember this Pentecost scene each Monday when we go to work, when we feel isolated or unappreciated, we'd be reminded of our work's value. It would help us understand that we never do our work alone; we are surrounded by the hymns and prayers of God's people. Anthems echo as we administer IVs, take an extra two minutes helping a customer, drive carefully, check on neighbors in our retirement complex, or repeatedly practice a new idea with a learning-disabled child. Work is our daily way to praise our God.

The Wind of God was blowing at Holy Trinity on Pentecost —
    blowing hard enough to distract worshippers from routine,
    bending people to their knees,
    moving people out of their pew places to minister,
    stirring up prayers and compassionate tears,
    showing how Sunday work and Monday work go hand-in-hand,
    providing the gift of eternal life at the altar, and the skills to
        mend this temporal life in the pews.
"The Spirit of God is like the wind," the pastor preached, "Recognize God's presence in the actions of people around you."

End notes

12 Rossetti, Christina *Rossetti.* Everyman's Library Pocket Poets. p.143. Alfred A. Knopf. New York, Toronto. 1993.

...in acknowledgment

I've written this book because of several sets of people who have formed gathered communities for me. One unique, long-distance community has been formed by teams of pastors and lay leaders from Lutheran congregations scattered from North Carolina to California, and from Minnesota to Texas. These are people who worked with me to test out the theory that ministry in daily life could be an organizing principle for congregational renewal. The Evangelical Lutheran Church in America's Division for Ministry (ELCA-DM) asked me to develop a continuing education program for rostered people that was based on that theory. The idea was generated by a cross-section of ELCA members, guided by two ELCA staff, Sally Simmel and Bob Sitze. A generous grant from Lutheran Brotherhood funded the project.

We worked with teams from several congregations at a time, first spending a weekend together. We then gathered for one-day sessions — first six months, then one year, later. In between times, the teams took concepts with which we had wrestled, and found practical ways to apply them in their own congregations. We learned together, shared ideas, and celebrated the growth in faith we witnessed. The concepts in this book are ones we formulated together; many of the ideas and stories are from these team members' experiences. The result is **SPLASH! The Ripples of the Baptized**, an ELCA continuing education program.

Others will recognize their names and stories here, too. I have been part of loving congregations since I was a small child. Contentious ones, too, but full of loving people. I've been part of the ministry of nine pastors during my lifetime. I cannot begin to count the number of lay people who have shared their faith with me, encouraged me, or showed me what the Christian life was all about. They have been Gospel-carriers to me.

If I did not love the church and believe in its power to serve God's will, I would not have taken the trouble to pick away at things many of us have long taken for granted. If I hadn't been challenged to look at the church through the lens of daily life, I probably never would have shaken out my old assumptions — or realized the powerful way lay people have enriched my faith. For both the challenge and the host of witnesses, I thank God.